WOMEN
AND
OTHER
MONSTERS

WOMEN AND OTHER MONSTERS

BUILDING A NEW MYTHOLOGY

JESS ZIMMERMAN

BEACON PRESS
BOSTON, MA

BEACON PRESS
Boston, Massachusetts
www.beacon.org

Beacon Press books
are published under the auspices of
the Unitarian Universalist Association of Congregations.

24 23 22   8 7 6 5 4 3 2

This book is printed on acid-free paper that meets the uncoated paper
ANSI/NISO specifications for permanence as revised in 1992.

Text design and composition by Kim Arney

Illustrations by Samira Ingold

Excerpt from "Myth" in *The Collected Poems of Muriel Rukeyser*
Copyright © 2005 by Muriel Rukeyser
Reprinted by permission of ICM Partners

Library of Congress Cataloging-in-Publication Data
Names: Zimmerman, Jess, author.
Title: Women and other monsters : building a new mythology /
Jess Zimmerman.
Description: Boston, MA : Beacon Press, [2021] | Includes bibliographical
references and index.
Identifiers: LCCN 2020045208 (print) | LCCN 2020045209 (ebook) |
ISBN 9780807055540 (paperback) | ISBN 9780807054987 (ebook)
Subjects: LCSH: Self-esteem in women. | Misogyny. | Monsters. |
Mythology, Greek.
Classification: LCC BF697.5.S46 Z54 2020 (print) | LCC BF697.5.S46
(ebook) | DDC 155.3/3382—dc23
LC record available at https://lccn.loc.gov/2020045208
LC ebook record available at https://lccn.loc.gov/2020045209

For Grammy

CONTENTS

A NOTE TO THE READER

THIS BOOK IS CALLED *Women and Other Monsters*. We'll get into what "monsters" means—we'll spend the whole book getting into that, really—but first, a quick note on the word "women." I use the term in its broadest possible sense, encompassing people who identify as women (regardless of assigned gender at birth) and people who have at some point been seen and treated as women (regardless of current gender). At issue is less the experience of feeling like a woman or knowing yourself as a woman, whatever that may mean to you, but of facing the assumptions and expectations and limitations placed on women under patriarchy.

If you were raised and socialized as a girl, if the people around you tried to prepare you from an early age for life as a woman, this book is for you, even if you turned out not to be a woman after all. If your body or presentation causes people to react to you as a woman, or to react to you in ways that are influenced by the cultural opinion of women, this book is for you—although trans women and nonbinary people face additional expectations, restrictions, and oppressions that I may not always cover. And honestly, if you were socialized and are responded to and identify as a man, you may find something here for you too. One of the consequences of living in a profoundly misogynistic society is that it's considered insulting to men to be compared to women. Even men who have always been seen as men may have been told their anger or sadness or sexuality was somehow too feminine. If that's you, although this book isn't written with you in mind, it isn't intended to shut you out.

I'm not a classicist, and my intention here isn't to offer the most authentic interpretation of these monsters. In some (probably most) cases, their metaphorical weight in the book will be different from the role they played in ancient Greek society. Here, their image, as it survives today, is being used as a framework for discussing women's current-day cultural role. The list of works cited and consulted include a few suggestions if you want to know what the original chroniclers or the scholars have to say.

Finally, a lot has been written on the use of "we" in essays. It's true it can be used to make sweeping statements sound grand instead of simplistic. I know not everyone will feel like a part of every "we." But it's always been an important pronoun to me, both in writing and editing: an acknowledgment that the greater work is a group project. There's no writing without a reader, so you and I are automatically a "we"—and on a personal level, I've always tried to write my way towards an understanding of what it means to be a human, in this culture, in this time. I hope that it doesn't feel like false solidarity, and that if you feel excluded from one "we," the next one will feel familiar to you.

SISTER MONSTERS

THE FIRST THING you saw when entering the *Dangerous Beauty* exhibit at the Metropolitan Museum of Art was a vintage dress from Versace's 1992–1993 "Miss S&M" collection. Straps of quilted leather crisscrossed the throat and décolletage of a headless mannequin, each strap adorned with a dollar-sized brassy coin bearing the head of a howling Gorgon, a play on Versace's usual logo of a placid Medusa face. The overall effect was oddly militaristic, a sort of four-star dominatrix look.

The exhibit, subtitled "Medusa in Classical Art," was tiny, tucked away in a single room in the mezzanine of the Greek and Roman art collection, next to the study gallery. So perhaps the dress was there to grab the attention of tourists who might accidentally have wandered up from the floor below, a broad indoor courtyard across which a young Hercules, lion-skin coat held meaningfully over his arm, stares impatiently at a statue of his older self. This is often the purpose, after all, of women's bodies and the clothing that adorns them, especially clothing that highlights the body's constraints. Clothing like this exists to catch the eye.

In this case, though, gawkers lured by "Miss S&M" were deposited into a room full of artifacts depicting not only Medusa but a coven of other female creatures of antiquity. Gorgon faces—both horrible ancient ones, with tusks and beards, and later ones, whose placid classical symmetry is broken only by a few demure snakes at the temples—stared out from roof tiles, armor, cups, and cameos. A piece of pottery showed Scylla with her snake legs splayed, a pack of dog heads lunging out of her crotch. Sirens perched their bird bodies on plates and mirrors. On the side of one shallow goblet, a Sphinx was painted in loving miniature, crouching over a male victim who appeared to plead for his life. Chasing after the female torso in her chic bondage, in other words, landed you in a nest of monsters.

The sixty pieces in the exhibit were intended to track the way Medusa and her counterparts became subject, despite their monstrousness, to principles of beauty. A gold pendant with a Gorgon's face from 450 BCE showed a grimacing creature with sharp teeth, a protruding tongue, a creased brow, a knobby chin. An exquisite nineteenth-century cameo, displayed in the same case, showed a perfect, precise neoclassical profile— which is to say, she looked a bit like Graham Chapman, but that was the style at the time. Apart from a coil of snake at the crown of her head, like a fascinator, and another knotted scarflike beneath her chin, she had no visible markers of monstrousness. You'd easily mistake her for a proper young lady with Bohemian hair and odd taste in accessories—the youngest *Downton Abbey* daughter, maybe. A Siren on one oil vessel from the sixth century BCE sported a full beard, though Sirens were generally coded as female, and had no arms; its head sat atop an awkward, turkey-like bird body. Catty-corner was a 1910 French woodcut in which a Siren, despite having developed bear arms and a fish tail to go with her wings, was still depicted as a beautiful bare-breasted feminine figure with a crown of flowing hair. Creatures conceived as repulsive were gradually reimagined as appealing, even seductive—at least on the surface. The monstrosity remains, but it's no longer visible.

"In a society centered on the male citizen, the feminization of monsters served to demonize women," writes curator Kiki Karoglou in an accompanying bulletin. The later monsters don't just look more beautiful and more feminine; they look more *human*, underscoring the idea that monstrousness is somehow the human woman's natural condition. As monsters became more pleasing to the eye, they were defanged—beauty being equated, in classical Greece, with moral goodness—and, paradoxically, made more dangerous. A Medusa with tusks, whiskers, and a grotesque distended tongue could be easily pegged as a threat; a human-looking Medusa could fly under the radar, until you tried to brush her hair. The resulting girl-faced beasts, read the exhibition text, foreshadow "the conceit of the seductive but threatening female that emerges in the late nineteenth century in reaction to women's empowerment." When a feminine face might belong to a secret Gorgon, any woman could be a monster. Perhaps every woman was.

This is one of the legacies we've inherited from the classical era, which underpins so much of what Westerners see as "culture" and "civilization": a suspicion of women in general, a feeling that every one of them may have claws and tails if you look below the waterline. The monsters massed together in this little room at the Met represented a series of cautionary tales. Women may look harmless on the face, they said, but look at their snake hair and dog crotches and claws. Look at them crouched over a male victim, ready to bite. Beware their ambition, their ugliness, their insatiable hunger, their ferocious rage.

It was these cautionary tales that brought me to the Met, shortly before the exhibit closed in January 2019. I was writing about these same female monsters, and a few others from the same period—specifically how they're used to represent qualities that women are supposed to tone down, lest we be seen as dangerous or grotesque. I wanted to look them in the face, all these Sphinxes and Gorgons. I wanted to be surrounded by them, and see if there was a place among them for me. Because my project was to rehabilitate these monsters—not externally, like the (male) artists who gradually made their forms more pleasing and symmetrical, but by showing how the traits we were told made them dangerous are actually their greatest strengths, and ours.

All the stories about monstrous women, about creatures who are too gross, too angry, too devious, too grasping, too smart for their own good, are stories told by men. The versions of these myths, the ones that are most familiar, come from Ovid, Homer, Hesiod, Virgil, Sophocles. I came to the Met to wonder what stories the monsters themselves would tell. What would Medusa say about the ugliness she first experienced as an unjust punishment, and then learned to use as a weapon? What happens when we free the Sphinx from the drama of Oedipus, and let her exist as something more than an obstacle to a man? What was it like for the Sirens on their lonely rock, watching everyone who tried to love them drown?

❧

I've had a long-standing interest in female heroes, the women who have broken through gendered notions of who is allowed to embody valor and strength, and I was beginning to suspect that monsters, perhaps ironically, could offer a whole new approach to heroism for people (like me) who are often tripped up by feminine ideals. The qualities we hail as heroic in Western culture—courage and fortitude, selflessness and nobility, steadiness of mind and will—are not unique to men. Arguably, they're not even characteristic. But in the male-dominated myth, folklore, and literature that defines our culture, they've been annexed as "masculine" traits. We're still struggling to create or consume stories about valorous women, unless they also display the "feminine" virtues: passive sex appeal and fragility that requires rescue. In a hero, these are flaws. Thus, any heroine who tries to embody both contains the seeds of her own undoing.

The female hero can hoist up the shackles of femininity and take them with her on adventures, but that's not the same as breaking free. (Think of that internet video of a fluffy dog running around a restaurant inside his plastic cage, pushing it along with his nose at an astonishing clip as his owner tries to keep up. You can drag your cage around, but it's still a cage.) In college, I was a particular fan of Edmund Spenser's "martial maid" Britomart, who gets to wear armor and carry a spear and go on quests and even rescue maidens—but eventually, even Britomart gallops back into her role as a princess, a wife, and the mother of a race of noble Britons. Her whole mission, in general, has been to find the man she glimpsed in a magic mirror and fell in love with. The rescuing damsels part was just a side quest.

Jumping ahead only a few centuries, Leeloo in the movie *The Fifth Element* is perhaps my favorite example of the heroine undone by her own femininity. She's conceived as a perfect being with inhuman skills in both fighting and intellect, but she spends most of the movie in a little Borat swimsuit—and in the end, she needs to be both physically rescued by a man and given purpose by his sexual interest. (Her ability to save the universe is neutralized until Korben says he loves her, and let's be honest, he's not talking about their deep emotional connection. They barely know each other, and Leeloo speaks no human language! She's *very* hot though.) We're not in 1590 anymore, or even 1997, and things are improving for the female hero. But truly transcending the cultural expectations placed on a woman—to be attractive and sexually available (but not too available), to never outshine the male heroes, to let herself be transformed at the end into a prize—is so rare that when it happens, we often regard it with suspicion. What do you *mean* Furiosa and Mad Max never bone down? This is a *movie!*

And if the heroine truly slips the constraints that her femininity is supposed to place on her, the very heroic virtues she embodies often mutate into monstrosity. In the Old English epic poem *Beowulf*, the eponymous male hero is described as an *aglæca*, a word for which we do not know the exact meaning but which is usually translated as something like "hero" or "warrior." Beowulf's antagonist, the monster Grendel, *also* gets described as an *aglæca*, which in his case is usually glossed as "demon" or "monster" or something similar. What the two have in common is the sense of being awe-inspiring or formidable, so that's probably more or less what *aglæca* means. But the word has a feminine form, *aglæcwif*, and the ancient text contains an *aglæcwif* too: Grendel's mother. There is no ambiguity to this word, not in the way it's come down to us; *aglæcwif* is translated as "monster-woman," "troll-lady," "wretch," or "hag." In other contexts, *"wif"* (which is also attached to other descriptors of Grendel's mother) specifically denotes a *human* woman, and yet—like it's not indignity enough that she's always called "Grendel's mother," as if the bards were Grendel's schoolmates who didn't realize mothers had names—the *aglæcwif* is assumed to be subhuman and bestial. She's just as much an *aglæca* as Beowulf, just as much a *wif* as the other human women to which that refers, but the combination inspires not awe but horror. The monstrousness of Grendel's mother, the factor that makes her a hag or a troll or a wretch, comes from her stepping outside the slim strictures of womanhood into the realm of *aglæca*, of formidability and awe. In another world, she would have been a hero.

❧

There were a few reasons I was interested in these particular monsters, the ones in the Met exhibit and their sisters in antiquity. The first is just that I dig them. I was raised on *D'Aulaires' Book of Greek Myths*. My childhood copy, which my parents still have, is missing both covers and parts of the index, and boasts several more full-color illustrations than other copies because I went to town on it with a marker when I was four. I went on to read Ovid and Homer and Sophocles in college and graduate school, but this was in part because their work is so foundational to other texts I wanted to study—which I knew mainly because my early *D'Aulaires'* obsession had primed me to recognize classical callbacks in literature and art. In other words, it all comes back to *D'Aulaires'*. This book can be traced back to a dorky pre-kindergartener in Velcro-closure KangaROOS, running shorts, and thick plastic-frame glasses, wandering around a museum in 1984 and identifying Greek gods by their iconography. (If this sounds like a brag, it's only because you can't see how silly my outfit looked.)

The second reason, which is related, is that other people dig them too. Almost every day while working on this book, I thought about a tweet from a user who changes usernames a lot but is currently @lilliesuperstar: "ok horse girls definitely had an energy but lets talk about the real powerhouses of middle school weird girls: the ancient mythology stans." It has, at the time of this writing, seventy thousand likes. Mythology obsessives are a powerful demographic, and right now, at least, it seems we find the monsters and villains particularly resonant. Of course I have a particular interest in the genre, but I have an enamel harpy pin on my purse, and I wrote this book on a laptop covered in monster stickers, often dressed in a pajama shirt with the Sphinx on it. The ability to buy something isn't the sole measure of its cultural worth, but I think it matters that someone was inspired enough by she-monsters to make each of these into a piece of art (the harpy pin was available in a three-pack with a Sphinx and a mermaid), and believed in their popularity enough to turn that art into a product.

For a less mercenary example, take Luciano Garbati's sculpture of Medusa with the severed head of Perseus, who—despite her swimsuit-model proportions and curiously blank pubis—became a popular feminist symbol in 2018, splashed across social media feeds to declare that women were fighting back. Also in 2018, Madeline Miller's *Circe*, a basically perfect novel that rehabilitates the enchantress who turns the hero's men into pigs in *The Odyssey*, was a major phenomenon and a best seller. *Circe* was not the first story of Greek antiquity to be revisited with the intent of putting sidelined or maligned women at the center. Margaret Atwood wrote *The Penelopiad*, from the perspective of Odysseus's wife, back in 2005. But a decade-plus later, we were done with long-suffering abandoned women. We were hungry for stories like *Circe*, which shook a villainess free from the minds of men and gave her a voice of her own. The mythology stans were out for blood.

Finally, I focused on these monsters because classical antiquity is called classical for a reason. It's a name bestowed by people who thought all the best—and *highest-class*—ideas, aesthetics, and ethics came from the five or six centuries on either side of Zero CE. The attitude may seem quaint now, but its influence lingers. The images and myths of antiquity influenced the art we still elevate, the literature that's disproportionately taught in schools, even our language. Many of the monsters I'll be writing about have snaked their way into the general vocabulary, metaphorically referring to a certain type of person or problem rather than the creature itself. When a woman is called a "harpy" or a "gorgon" or (less disparagingly) a "screen siren," when you are caught "between Scylla and Charybdis," when a problem that gets worse the more you try to fix it is a "hydra," when an unsolvable question is "the riddle of the Sphinx," that is evidence of the outsized influence of classical lore. The monsters in this book are part of the mythos that influenced the current dominant culture as it was being built. These are the bedtime stories patriarchy tells itself.

There are other monstrous women in folklore, from traditions that are less overrepresented in the white/male/Western cultural juggernaut—and some of them will show up here. The ones that organize the book, though, are from Greek antiquity, not because they're the most interesting stories but because they're complicit. I'm not interested in elevating these myths but in analyzing them: how they function as tight little packages of expectation seeded into the culture and how they can be subverted.

❧

Jeffrey Jerome Cohen, the humanities professor who literally wrote the book on "monster theory," outlines seven defining characteristics, or theses, of the monster. Some are pretty academic, but a few are immediately resonant: "the monster dwells at the gates of difference" and "the monster polices the borders of the possible." Monsters are signposts, in other words, to separate acceptable from unacceptable, what's allowed from what is not. Their monstrosity is deviation blown up to exaggerated size, the mythic equivalent of "If you keep doing that, your face will stick that way."

Monsters exist in opposition to normality: exaggeratedly large or small, too many limbs or too few eyes, too complex or too rudimentary. Monstrosity is relative, born in the gulf between the expectation and the reality. Even Godzilla could live happily in a Godzilla-scale Tokyo.

But if the expectations are too narrow, nearly anything can become monstrous. If you are only allowed to be tiny, it is grotesque to be medium. If you are only allowed to be quiet, it is freakish to be loud. The more you are circumscribed, the easier it is to deviate, and the more deviation comes to seem outlandish or even dangerous.

For women, the boundaries of acceptability are strict, and they are many. We must be seductive but pure, quiet but not aloof, fragile but industrious, and always, always small. We must not be too successful, too ambitious, too independent, too self-centered—and when we can't manage all the contradictory restrictions, we are turned into grotesques. Women have been monsters, and monsters have been women, in centuries' worth of stories, because stories are a way to encode these expectations and pass them on.

We've built a culture on the backs of these monstrous women, letting them prop up tired morals about safety and normalcy and feminine propriety. But the traits they represent—aspiration, knowledge, strength, desire—are not hideous. In men's hands, they have always been heroic.

The monsters of myth have been stationed at those borders in order to keep us out; they are intended as warnings about what happens when women aspire beyond what we're allowed. A monster like Grendel's mother polices the borders of *aglæca*, shows you what happens if the wrong people get in. The she-beasts in this book patrol other borders, other gates: ambition, intellect, complexity, power, pride. They mark areas on a map: Do not enter. Here be monsters.

But if stepping outside the boundaries makes you monstrous, that means monsters are no longer bound. What happens if we charge through the gates and find that living on the other side—in all our Too Muchness, oversized and overweening and overcomplicated as we are—means living fully for the first time? Then the monster story stops being a warning sign, and starts to be a guide.

Draw a new map. Mark down: Be monsters here.

HOW TO TURN
A MAN TO STONE

OF ALL THE THINGS I miss about the early internet—the quietness of it, the way Nazis stayed mostly out of the public discourse, the fact that nobody had really yet figured out how to sell users as products—perhaps the greatest loss is usernames. There are still parts of Online where you routinely go by a sobriquet (Tumblr mostly), but by and large, we're all going by some variation of our given names. When I was young, this was practically unheard of. Instead you chose a name that foregrounded some part of yourself, a pop culture reference or a fantasy persona or at least "hot-2trot69." By the time I was in college, I had picked up some self-hyping usernames, but in high school, the words I chose to encapsulate my entire online identity usually had something to do with physical or sexual insufficiency. It didn't occur to me to highlight a part of myself that didn't have to do with being worthless as an object. What could be more important?

One of these was "Xenon," not because of its cool cyberpunk resonance but because a guy I'd been sleeping with had told me we had "no chemistry." (Get it?) Another was "Medusa." This was because I was a Greek myth nerd, a little bit, but mostly it was because Medusa is famously ugly. In myth, she was one of the three Gorgon sisters, all of whom were famed for being so grotesque that looking directly at them would turn you to stone. They had wings and tusklike teeth and brazen claws; snakes wrapped around their bodies and grew from their heads instead of hair. Of the three, only Medusa was mortal, which is of course why we remember her name; as always in myth, women win their fame by dying. But her mortality and eventual death wasn't the point for me. The point was her legendary hideousness, so profound that nobody could even approach her.

This is being a teenage girl in microcosm: I had bad skin, didn't know how to wear makeup, and was too fat to look good in a prom dress, not that I tried, so I must be *so ugly that to merely look upon me meant certain death*. It's a dramatic time of life. And truth be told, even then I knew going by "Medusa" was audacious. It was a jaded shrug, an attempt to recuse myself from the game of human attraction before anyone pointed out that I'd already lost. What better defense against being considered insufficiently beautiful than to stake a claim on definitive, unassailable, remarkable ugliness? But every time I logged in, I felt a little intimidated by my own swagger. Medusa and the other Gorgons were hideous in a way that went far beyond not being pretty. What was I thinking, aligning myself with Medusa—not an ugly woman but *the* ugly woman, the avatar of ugly power? Medusa doesn't just fail to measure up; she turns ugliness into a weapon. She's so ugly it hurts—but it doesn't hurt her first.

What would it mean for ugliness to be not a vulnerability but a strength? At the time I couldn't even fathom it. I was trying to signal a surrender: *Yes, I know how I look.* But it didn't feel humble. It felt ostentatious. I was trying to acknowledge not being pretty, but in the process, I was claiming something much greater, something I hadn't earned: ugliness, and the power that comes with it. What made me uncomfortable about calling myself "Medusa," though I probably couldn't have articulated it then, was the knowledge that ugliness was *active*, and it was an action I didn't yet have the courage to take. I was shut out from beauty by forces outside my control—by the people and the social systems that make the rules. But being outside of beauty is not the same as being ugly, any more than being outside of Congress means you're an anarchist. Ugliness was something I would have to define and stake out for myself.

I've tried to do so, not always successfully, for the twenty-five or so years since. And what I've learned is that ugliness is more than just the absence of beauty. It's not failing to conform to the rules—it's an active embracing of chaos. Helen of Troy's face might have launched a thousand ships, but one look from Medusa could have sent them all to the bottom, weighted down with a crew of stones.

I suspect we all have a particular monstrousness that we blame for everything wrong in our lives. This is mine. I have always, on some level, believed that if I'd been prettier, I would have also been happier, more successful, more loved, more fulfilled. This conviction was especially strong in my teens, back when I was logging in as Medusa. Being a teenage girl is dramatic in part because it's your first, chilliest dunking in the certain knowledge that your body is your worth. I'd been a chubby kid, and so the idea that my body was a source of shame wasn't new to me, but previously I'd only been a disappointment to my family. Now, I was understanding that an unbeautiful woman is an unfulfilled promise to the world.

I realize now that some of this is illusion—that those promises were made on my behalf, without my input, by people who didn't have my best interests at heart. But I've never gotten over the bone-deep certainty that my failure to be beautiful is the secret root of all my other flaws. I've felt dogged by the impossible, beautiful, never-born version of myself, the one who is consequently beloved and secure and courageous and, when she is not, given generous amounts of patience and care.

The worst thing about this belief is that it's true. Beauty is demonstrably a cheat code for a slightly easier life—people just a little more likely to do you a favor, love just a little easier to access, the world just a little more welcoming. (This is not to say that beautiful people have no problems, but they don't have *this* one.) You're likely to be given more opportunities and more benefit of the doubt if you fit the thin, white, young, able-bodied beauty ideal.

We've known for decades the effect that beauty has on the way we're perceived, not only in terms of sexual or aesthetic value but in terms of morals, charm, intellect, and talent. Studies as far back as the 1970s have demonstrated the halo effect of attractiveness: Beautiful people are judged to be happier, smarter, more successful, better parents, deeper thinkers, more creative. There is rarely a day when I don't wonder what my life would have been like under that halo. When I encounter someone talented and successful in writing or art, who is also exceptionally beautiful—or at least in the neighborhood—my appreciation of their work carries an indelible bitter tang. *Well of course,* I say to myself, every time. *If I'd looked like that, I might have believed in myself too. I might have tried harder. I might have spent less time berating myself for my flaws. People would have given me a chance, and thought I was good. I would have given myself a chance.* I am being ridiculous when I think this, but I'm not wrong.

Beauty is currency, and as with all currency we are relentlessly capitalistic about it. Sometimes this equation, beauty for money, is literal: it's something you can buy, and don't let anyone pretend it isn't. All those curiously ageless actresses didn't get their perpetual youth for free. And it's something you can be paid for: there are entire professions built on beauty. If you're beautiful and lucky, it can make you a living. If you're very lucky, it can make you rich. But beauty is also metaphorical currency, an asset that can be traded for goods and goodwill, for attention and forbearance. You can tell how close you are to beauty by how much is handed to you— both actual freebies and less tangible gifts, deference and priority and tolerance and care. If you're close to it, and you think nothing is handed to you, that's only because you don't know what it's like to be further away.

Ugliness, by contrast, will never be a currency. But money is not the only route to power.

❧

Medusa was beautiful once. Not everyone knows this, but it's all there in Ovid's *Metamorphoses.* The only mortal Gorgon was originally a mortal woman, whose splendid hair was so alluring that it captured the interest of Poseidon, the god of the sea. Some mealymouthed translators refer to what happened next as Medusa being "ravished" or even "rifled," but let's be clear: Poseidon liked her hair, so he raped her. Gods are used to getting what they want, no matter how fleetingly they want it.

The rape took place in Athena's temple, and Athena, it must be admitted, has never been much of a friend to her fellow women. The warlike goddess of wisdom, who wasn't even *gestated* by a woman (she sprang fully grown from her father's head), is the original "not like the other girls" girl. Outraged by the defilement of her sacred space, and absolutely uninterested in assigning fault to her uncle, she turned Medusa's famous tresses into snakes. This is the double-edged sword of female beauty: Those who fail at it are less than human, but those who succeed are punished and shamed.

Ugliness can make you vulnerable, but so can beauty. That mark we're all trying to hit, the one that makes you favored, the one that makes you visible, is a target set by men's disdain and men's desire. Even when you're not trying to attract a man sexually, even when you want nothing to do with men *or* sex, our cultural aesthetic values for women are maddeningly inextricable from the penchants of powerful men. Thinness isn't considered beautiful because it's objectively good, but because it signals abstemiousness and fragility and a dedication to staying small. The kind of men who have been in a position to influence the culture like these things. Whiteness is considered beautiful because these same men have gross ideas about race and "purity." Big eyes and smooth skin are considered beautiful because of their connection to fertile and pliable youth. To fail to conform is dangerous because it locks you out of a world built to cater to the whims of such men. But to succeed is dangerous, too, because it locks you into a space framed by appetite. Much later, after Medusa's death, Athena is said to have given the doctor Asclepius two drops of the Gorgon's blood—one a universal panacea, the other a deadly poison. This is how beauty works: a toxin and a cure.

Ovid's story focuses on the snake hair, but we must assume there was something more to Athena's unjust curse, because really the snakes are the least of Medusa's worries. Older images of the Gorgons also have tusks, scales, and often beards. Medusa's transformation was a complete erasure of everything that had seemed to give her value: her hair, her beautiful face, her potential as a victim or a prize. But Athena's mistake was that she didn't just take Medusa's beauty; she handed her ugliness, which isn't the same thing at all. Her new face, Medusa found, had gained the power to petrify. In losing everything, she had become a weapon herself.

In a just world, Medusa would have mounted Olympus and turned Athena into a not-like-other-girls rock. But the world is not just, and gods are gods, however corrupt. Instead, she visited death on every challenger on Earth. She became a demigod, a legend, a monster, and the mother of monsters. Beauty had not protected her; ugliness was her armor and her blade.

People look through your face, or past it, when there's nothing there they want. They're not afraid to meet your eyes—they just don't see the point.

Better for them to be afraid. Better for them to think they'll turn to stone.

❦

The word "monster" comes from the Latin *monstrum*, meaning an omen or a portent—a deformed human or animal infant whose birth, because it was atypical, was understood to be a sign. A sign of what? In the case of the two-headed calf born in Saxony in 1522, it was a sign of a schism within the church led by Martin Luther. The famous and possibly fictitious Monster of Ravenna, a horned and winged infant with an eye in the middle of its single claw-footed leg, was fingered as a portent of any number of battles, malfeasances, and religious upheavals, including Luther again. And always, especially in the sixteenth through eighteenth centuries, the monstrous birth was indicative of a mother's secret sin. Physical exaggerations might indicate the mother's outsize passions or covert lusts.

Our reaction to this kind of ugliness—to deviation from the supposedly correct form—hasn't changed much, considering that we've had centuries to sort it out. Deformity is still considered a sign of inner evil: Richard III's twisted back, but also, hundreds of years later, Count Rugen's sixth finger and Voldemort's flat reptilian nose. You can tell a lot about what a culture considers deformed by looking at its villains. They're more likely to be disabled in some way but also more likely to be dark, old, fat, or fey. And one of the things that's immediately obvious is that the threshold for women's ugliness is very, very low. It's sufficient to look like Helena Bonham Carter but just not ever brush your hair.

For many of us, one of our earliest exposures to the idea of ugliness is the ugly stepsisters in Cinderella. The redhead in the old Disney cartoon looks a little like me: round cheeks, crinkly nose, nasolabial folds, drawn-on eyebrows. My hair is cooler, but at least she's not fat. Neither of us is offensive to the eye, but that's never been what matters; both of us have too little of some things and, crucially, too much of others. In the Disney cartoon, the sisters' big feet (I have these too) don't fit into the glass slipper, and that's it: they are out of the running to marry the prince. In the original Brothers Grimm story, as most people now know, that's only the beginning. The ambitious sisters won't give up on royal matrimony that easily. One cuts off her toes and the other her heel, and it's only the blood dripping out of the slipper that gives them away. When standards are impossibly narrow, you mutilate yourself to fit.

The sisters in the Grimm story aren't ugly. In fact, they're described as beautiful. Maybe that's why they're primed to hack off parts of themselves to conform to an arbitrary mold. Disney's big-footed would-be brides gamely shove their clodhoppers into the delicate shoe, but it's clear that no amount of contortion or surgery will make it work: they're too outsized, too grotesque, and ultimately, that's what sets them free. They may not live happily ever after, but at least their feet are whole. When you're so tantalizingly close, though, why not slice off a sliver of heel?

Ideals of beauty are Cinderella's slipper—or, to wander back towards Medusa's place and time, the bed of Procrustes, who would stretch or dismember his guests to make them fit his accommodations. Your options are usually no more than two: torture yourself into compliance or walk away. Walking away *is* an alternative, sort of. You can't stop people from reacting to you within the beauty framework, evaluating whether you qualify and treating you accordingly, but you do have the option of trying very hard not to care. But there's something about beauty that deranges you the closer you approach, like some science-fiction monolith. Once you get a taste of its power, you want to claim it, even as it recedes from you. And if you lie down on that Procrustean bed, you will suffer until you conform.

Like 22 million other people, I spent a little time in 2014 playing *Kim Kardashian: Hollywood*, the mobile game based (in the very loosest sense) on the public persona of professional public persona Kim Kardashian. In-world, according to the dialogue and plot of the game, *KKH* is entirely predicated on beauty: the cartoon character you pilot is a model rising through the ranks of celebrity, using game money and sometimes real money to pay for ever-fancier outfits, hair, and accessories, which in turn give you bonuses in your job (mostly clicking a button that says "Pose") and your personal life (clicking a button that says "Flirt"). Outside of the game narrative, in real life, *KKH* is actually predicated on your ability to ferociously waste your time doing the same gestures over and over, in exchange for benefits that only hold any value when you're inside the game with its very particular rules and economy. In other words, it's beauty incarnate.

In *KKH*, you win money and influence by tapping buttons with labels like "Smile," "New Pose," "Check Makeup," or "Perfect Lighting." That's for modeling challenges, anyway. Like Kim herself, the game allows you to expand into ventures like reality TV, dating people ideally more famous than you, or creating and marketing an app. Regardless, the mechanism is the same: Hit buttons until you run out of energy, then wait to get more, then hit buttons again. (The animation is also the same—whatever option you tap, your character stands around saucily, periodically looking at her fingernails. The tapping is the point.) The most successful players are the ones who funnel in the most attention or the most funds: either putting real money into the app or setting alarms to alert them when their energy is refilled and it's time to tap again. In exchange for your focused ministrations, you win cash and fans—virtual cash and fans, of course, worthless outside of the game, but within the game, the only thing that matters.

There are lots of mobile games like this, which train you to perform compulsive actions in order to maximize rewards that are only given value by the game. Although not all of them are such *obvious* metaphors for the pursuit of beauty, they're metaphors all the same. Feminine beauty is a game you play for imaginary points that only matter in the game, a set of repetitive and often self-perpetuating actions—concealer to cover pimples caused by concealer, deep conditioner to soften hair made brittle by bleach, and let's not even talk about damage to your metabolism caused by dieting—undertaken with dogged devotion for intangible rewards. You can opt out—lose all your points and progress, but at least be free of the obligation—but you must opt out completely. You can choose not to play the game, but you can't choose not to click and still be playing. (As with beauty, there are many available subplots and strategies in *KKH* that I've simply avoided entirely. In life, I choose not to fuck with high-heeled shoes, for instance, and in *KKH*, I have always resisted buying a winery. But when I was playing, I still tapped. You have to *tap*.)

In the case of beauty, though, everyone is playing. *Everyone* is playing. There's no app to close—if you stop participating, if you cancel every waxing appointment and quit your diet and stop putting on mascara day after day after day, you just stop accruing points. It's hard to even know how to try to stop. It's hard to want to. There's a reason we call these clicker games addictive. The repetition itself, the striving and occasional reward, is the first tendril of obsession. And then there's the sunk cost: *If I stop now, I lose everything, because what I've built only matters as long as I accept and live within this fictional world.* The rewards you get for diligent gameplay are fake, but they're fake the way money is fake: a consensual delusion scaffolded only by our own agreement to behave as though it's real. Try to live outside the fiction and see how far you get.

☙

By a lot of standards, I'm extraordinarily lucky. I happen to have the skin color (white) and the basic facial features (European) that my culture prizes. I'm even blue-eyed and blondeish, under the dye: a surprisingly Aryan specimen, considering my 100-percent-Jewish background. I don't have visible disabilities, which many people still react to like superstitious medieval peasants. I'm on the tall side. I'm only middle-aged. If I were a man, I wouldn't be writing this. But for women, the "correct" form is so narrowly defined that almost anyone's physical form can be deviant. We don't have to have two heads to be monstrous. It's enough to have two chins.

Being fat—I have always been fat—is the main thing that made me feel fundamentally freakish. (Although this is compounded, now, by aging. Like many people who have believed essentially from birth that they're aesthetically offensive, I've found in retrospect that sometimes I was actually pretty cute—but of course, that was always *then*. Now I have *jowls*.) There's no shortage of people volunteering to tell fat women we don't count as women, or as humans. Even the nineties-era backlash slogan "real women have curves" posited that some women are more "real" than others—a slightly different set of women, of course, but still one that emphatically disqualifies whole swaths of women from "realness," including me. I don't "have curves"; I am fat, and not in a cute smooth body-positive way but in a lumpy, cellulite-y, stretch-marked way. In many ways, it's the *most* human kind of fatness—a fatness that succumbs to tension and gravity, that transcends nothing. But the feminine beauty ideal has no truck with this kind of humanity, the fleshy kind. To be considered human, instead of monster, you need to overshoot and land in the realm of the ethereal. This is absolutely not possible for me, a lumpy bundle of flesh rubbed raw on the edges. Indeed, no matter how beautiful I find many fat women, it's not possible for any of us. Fatness alone, these days, is enough to lock you out of the citadel. Go back a few centuries and they'd let you in—but then the thinner women would be left outside banging on the door (along, of course, with everyone considered too dark). It's a tiny place, beauty. There's only room for a few.

On top of being fat, I have large coarse feet and hands, thick ankles, thin frizzy hair, a plump and aging neck, usually at least one zit, eyebrows somehow simultaneously sparse and overgrown, skin so dry I scratch holes into it during winter if it doesn't crack on its own. Some of these various infelicities are self-inflicted. I bit my nails to the quick for most of my life, and I still tear up my fingers and cuticles when I'm stressed, which is all of the time. Pulling out my eyebrows is a stress reaction, too, and hair-pulling, and picking at zits. It's easy to deface your body when you've always seen it as an adversary, or an anchor weighing you down.

I am not that far from the thin-white-abled-young beauty ideal—two out of four—but I am far enough. Thinness is *very* important, thinness and its counterparts: delicacy, fragility. (It is in fact more important, in terms of the feminine ideal, to be fragile than to be perfectly healthy. Consider all the consumptive love interests of yore. You can be ill if you are ill in an elegant way.) I am the utmost opposite of delicate. Even apart from being fat, I have always had a certain indelible masculinity, no matter how I'm dressed and made up. A friend once said, "Even when you're wearing heels, you walk like you're wearing combat boots." It was intended, and taken, as a compliment, but it was definitely a compliment about something other than beauty. This alone—being fat, being a bit masculine, being in a word *hulking*—locks me out.

The Procrustean bed of beauty is unforgiving—and somehow, while those who make themselves fit are often turned into objects, those who don't are seen as something less than people. Sometimes I look at other women's hands clutching the pole on the subway, their tiny bones and fine soft translucent skin, and think: *If that's what human women look like, what am I?*

〜

Picture a car radio on a long highway in the middle of nowhere, static deforming and shifting as you twiddle the knob, sounding more like a human voice as you approach a signal and then breaking into cacophony again as you overshoot. That's what seeking beauty is like: trying to tune yourself, with minute precision, in a way that makes you audible to the world. The culturally determined wavelength that lets people see you clearly is so narrow, and the farther away you are, the more you dissolve into noise.

Maybe a better metaphor, since we're talking about the visual, is light: the few thin wavelengths of light that are visible to the human eye. More straightforwardly, a strip of light inside which things are illuminated, outside which they're dark. The idea is the same: in the darkness, in the infrared, in the ultrahigh frequency bands, you're too far from the target to even be perceived. Outside the ideal spectrum, among the fat and old and plain, eyes skate off you. People scan Tinder under the table when you sit down for your date. They forget you after the interview and hire someone else. When they talk about "women"—as in "How do I meet women?" or "Will there be women at the party?" but also as in "Women are always getting hit on and catcalled"—they don't mean you. That's the reason we're willing to struggle so hard to tune in to the narrow band of beauty. If beauty is a thin spear of light surrounded by darkness, then what lives in the darkness must be either ghosts—inconsequential, invisible—or monsters. Something to be reviled or ignored.

This is metaphorically true for all of us, but literally true for black women, since visual recording technology—like film and video cameras—is usually calibrated to white skin, expecting a white subject. The test images used to light-balance film cameras until the 1990s were pictures of white women. Emulsions on earlier Kodak film were optimized for light skin tones, and the company only added more sensitivity to darker ranges when companies demanded it for furniture. Dark-skinned models, actors, and regular people in vacation snaps may be literally invisible, or at least uninterpretable, to a camera set to a white default. The Polaroid cameras and film used to photograph people for their passbooks in apartheid South Africa deliberately made dark skin darker to the point of erasing the features entirely. "The absence of our likeness accurately rendered in photographs is one more piece of the construct of white supremacy," writes Syreeta McFadden in a 2014 *BuzzFeed News* article. "Film stocks that can't show us accurately help to control the narrative around appearance, and shapes our reality and the value of our lives in American society. If we are invisible, we are unvalued and inhuman. Beasts. Black bodies accepted as menacing, lit in ways that cloak our features in shadows."

This is not merely a technical quibble, McFadden writes, but a nonverbal manifesto on the value and deserved visibility of dark skin:

> I don't know when the first time was I learned that I was ugly. Or the part where I was taught to despise my dark skin, or the part where my mother's friends or old aunts yelled at us to stay out of the sun and not get so dark. I hear this from dark girls all the time. I don't know how we were taught to see a flattened blackness, to fear our own shades of dark. I do know how we accepted the narratives of white society to say that

dark skin must be pitied, feared, or overcome. There are overwhelming images of dark-skinned peoples in Western imagination that show us looking desperate, whipped, animalistic. Our skin blown out in contrast from film technologies that overemphasize white skin and denigrate black skin. Our teeth and our eyes shimmer through the image, which in its turn become appropriated to imply this is how black people are, mimicked to fit some racialized nightmare that erases our humanity.

Women who are immediately perceived as disabled, too, are vulnerable to a whole other level of invisibility. "I would listen to other kids my age talk about attraction in terms of a sliding scale—someone could be sexy or not, or sort of sexy, or not sexy before but kinda getting more sexy all of a sudden," writes Chloé Cooper Jones in a compelling essay on disability, attraction, and perception in *The Believer.* "My disability kept me, in the eyes of others, off that scale altogether, like an animal or a child. I saw people cringe when I referenced a crush or joined my girlfriends in lusting after a celebrity. I made people uncomfortable." Cooper Jones, who has a spinal disorder, frames her essay around a male acquaintance who told her—with winking, conspiratorial unearned intimacy—that he couldn't maintain an erection for any woman who wasn't "model-beautiful." "I saw that my body barred me from his realm of possible women," she writes. "What he reflected back wasn't kind, but it was clear. This is how men see me." She didn't say, but didn't need to, that while disabled men are also subject to a host of degradations and injustices, this particular experience—of being negated as an object of desire, and then effectively negated as a person *because* you are not desirable—is the province of women, because of the way our humanity has always been contingent on our beauty.

These additional invisibilities come layered on top of the invisibility imposed on women generally, especially women who are not understood as beautiful. There is no male-controlled culture that by default allows women to be seen. Some are more insistent and literal about this than others: there are nations where the mandate for female invisibility is so oppressive that face and head coverings, otherwise a personal expression of faith, have been made into mandatory expressions of subservience. In my country, women are occluded in subtler ways. We're obscured not by cloth but by disregard, by the way men are taught to devalue us and we are taught to devalue ourselves. It's only beauty—and specifically femininity, and even more specifically, sexual attractiveness to men—that burns through the fog. It's no wonder we'll kill ourselves chasing it. Beauty is a currency, but it's also a baseline: the place you have to stand to be noticed, the thing that makes you real.

All this means that historically, even our heroines—women who are, in all other ways, outside the norm—are subject to the demands of physical perfection. Take Gal Gadot in the 2017 film *Wonder Woman*. A powerful and principled female fighter raised on an isolated island of powerful, principled female fighters, an island that values strength and dedication and has never so much as encountered the male gaze—and yet she and every one of her fellow Amazons is willowy, symmetrical, high-cheekboned, youthful, and hairless from the neck down. We barely know how to envision a female hero who isn't. We only recently figured out how to envision one who's wearing clothes. If a woman is not beautiful, she must be invisible; if a woman is extraordinary, therefore, she must be beautiful. Who ever heard of an extraordinary ghost?

Few cultural properties have even tried to put forth a truly ugly heroine. In recent years, for instance, we've gotten to see television's version of George R. R. Martin's Brienne of Tarth, described as hideous in the novels but played onscreen by Gwendolyn Christie, who is just tall. Somewhat more transgressive is Furiosa of *Mad Max: Fury Road*, visibly disabled and stripped of her hair and other feminine signifiers, but still portrayed by Charlize Theron, perfect face and figure and all, under the motor-oil makeup. What would a heroine look like who truly embodied the unbeautiful wilderness? Would she have the Gorgon's beard or tusks, or something else entirely? We deserve her. But do we know how to imagine her? Would we know how to see her, if she appeared?

❧

Medusa lost her beauty—or rather, it was taken from her. Beauty is always something you can lose. Women's beauty is seen as something separate from us, something we owe but never own: We are its stewards, not its beneficiaries. We tend it like a garden where we do not live.

Oh, but ugliness—ugliness is always yours. Almost everyone has some innate kernel of grotesquerie. Even fashion models, I've heard, tend to look a bit strange and froggish in person, having been gifted with naturally level faces that pool light luminously instead of breaking it into shards. And everyone has the ability to mine their ugliness, to emphasize and magnify it, to distort even those parts of themselves that fall within acceptable bounds.

Where beauty is narrow and constrained, ugliness is an entire galaxy, a myriad of sparkling paths that lurch crazily away from the ideal. There are so few ways to look perfect, but there are thousands of ways to look monstrous, surprising, upsetting, outlandish, or odd. Thousands of stories to tell in dozens of languages: the languages of strong features or weak chins, the languages of garish makeup and weird haircuts and startling clothes, fat and bony and hairy languages, the languages of any kind of beauty that's not white. Nose languages, eyebrow languages, piercing and tattoo languages, languages of blemish and birthmark and scar. When you give up trying to declare yourself acceptable, there are so many new things to say.

"Beauty is in some way boring," the writer and scholar Umberto Eco said in a 2007 lecture on the history of ugliness. "Even if its concept changes through the ages, nevertheless, a beautiful object must always follow certain rules. So to speak: a beautiful nose shouldn't be longer than *that* or shorter than *that*. On the contrary, an ugly nose can be as long as the one of Pinocchio, as big as the one of an elephant, or like the beak of an eagle. Ugliness is unpredictable and offers an infinite range of possibilities. Beauty is finite; ugliness is infinite, like God." Like God, or like a demigod, or anyway, like a monster.

Ugliness is the negative space of beauty, everything that beauty doesn't allow. It's only in turning away from the tiny target that you see the infinite space surrounding it. You're not supposed to do this, of course. You're supposed to be ashamed of your ugliness. Why? Because it's objectively shameful? Or because it reduces your value as a decoration, a prize, an advertisement—because it benefits nobody but yourself?

Medusa lost her beauty, but she never lost her ugliness. It only grew and grew, becoming something greater than herself but still part of her legend. Becoming, in its own way, beautiful—but an undomesticated, frightening beauty, shaken loose from the drudgery of performing to expectations. When Medusa was eventually defeated—by a man, it's always by a man—two new beings sprang from her neck: the winged horse Pegasus, and Chrysaor, a giant with a golden sword. In some stories they're formed when drops of Gorgon blood hit the sea, but I've always thought of them more like pearls, roiling around inside Medusa as she wreaked her stony vengeance, little irritants collecting nacreous coats of poison blood and somehow growing spectacular. Could these brilliant creatures have been conceived under the claustrophobic constraints of beauty?

The freedom of ugliness includes the freedom to make a new kind of beauty, a kind that nobody's thought to denigrate or control—to create it out of your body and blood or out of the dirt or out of the stones of the people you petrify. If you stopped laboring over beauty for someone else to judge and find wanting, how much more energy would you have to cultivate your ugliness? To build something you can keep?

Medusa's reign didn't last forever, of course. Perseus showed up to slaughter her with an armload of magic items fit for a fairy tale. From Medusa's old tormentor Athena, he had a mirror-polished shield so he could observe her without looking her in the face. From Hades of the underworld, he had a cap of invisibility that hid him from view. From the smith Hephaestus, a sickle that could decapitate the monster. From Hermes the messenger, winged sandals that let him fly. That's what it took to kill her: the gods of wisdom and death and fire and flight all working together. Tricks and steel and stealth and speed, all stacked against the one weapon of ugliness.

Athena took the Gorgon's head from Perseus and mounted it on her breastplate, so that any foe would be petrified before the fight even began. (She was, you'll recall, the one who made Medusa hideous in the first place, the one who compounded her victimization by punishing her—so of course she also benefited from the power Medusa struggled and died for. The world had not suddenly become fair.) Athena was a goddess of strategy and skill, wisdom and statecraft, but she wasn't above wanting to feel pretty—she was among the competitors for Paris's golden apple, the one with "For the Fairest" printed on it, the one that started the Trojan War. But with all that proficiency, all that fairness, where did she turn for protection? To a legendarily ugly face, the ugliest face she could find. A face so ugly she'd had to make it, and kill it, and steal its power.

Mortal Greeks, too, wore the Gorgon on their shields: her tongue out, eyes and cheeks bulging, tusk teeth piercing through her rictus grin. They depicted her on doors or entryway tiles to stave off unwelcome guests. Her ugliness was an amulet against invasions large and small, a prayer for staying safe and staying whole.

And meanwhile, from Medusa's headless body, Pegasus sprang—the winged horse, which would long remain untamed. These are the components of ugliness: a warding symbol and a fantastical beast. Protection and unfettered, wild flight.

❧

Ugliness is larger than beauty, and accordingly, standards of ugliness go beyond beauty standards. The concept of ugliness has attached itself to race, class, disability, anything that veers from the self-appointed mainstream. In a landmark 1958 study cited in *Brown v. Board of Education*, black children rated black dolls as uglier, white ones as prettier, demonstrating the pervasive effects of a segregated and striated society. From the mid-nineteenth through twentieth centuries in the US, "unsightly beggar ordinances"— later shorthanded by scholars as Ugly Laws—sought to regulate the appearance in public spaces of people who were visibly disabled or destitute. Practically every nonwhite race, as well as many now considered white, has been caricatured into grotesquerie, their supposed repulsiveness standing in for the threat they posed to the ruling or colonizing class. Even people who hew in almost every way to imposed beauty standards may find themselves tripped up by these vicious, targeted notions of ugliness, intended to uphold Western patriarchal ideals by denigrating any deviation. I have a deaf friend, for instance, who is white, blonde, thin, pretty, and athletic but still struggles with the ingrained idea that deaf people are fundamentally less attractive. She's proof that the idea is demonstrably wrong, but it didn't come from a vacuum.

So the accusation of ugliness has been an ever-changing Protean weapon, wielded always against the most vulnerable: Medusa's face on Athena's shield, forced to protect her oppressor. Ugliness has always had power, but the power has been used to segregate and threaten and destroy. What happens if the Gorgon rises, not a shield for the status quo but its worst nightmare? What happens if Medusa takes back her power, her gift? If the ugly come for their own?

The closer you get to beauty, the more it recedes from you. You can approach it only asymptotically, narrowing but never closing the gap between your fallible human body and the ideal. The world's most poreless, slim, symmetrical woman can still get a zit or a patch of dry elbow skin. In other words, nobody *is* beautiful, or at least not beautiful enough that they feel they're finished and can relax. We merely strive towards beauty, which is not a state but an action. We understand beauty-as-action implicitly— it's a whole industry, after all. "Beauty products" are not for havers, but for seekers, the people battering the walls of the impenetrable city, trying to get in. So what is ugliness-as-action? What awaits us if we turn away from Eden and strike out the other way?

❧

I don't want to set myself up as some kind of prodigy of ugliness. Whatever I might feel looking at small hands on the subway, I am in fact only human, and humans have a hard time giving up on the dream of being widely loved. (And who knows what loneliness Medusa endured after her transformation and before she took her anger out on the world? Even Gorgons might consider trading power for acceptance.) I know what's expected of me, the rules of the game and the rewards with their fictional value, and I can't give all of it up, not yet. Plus, these days one of the primary things working against me is my age—our cultural idea of beauty is very much predicated on youth—which means fully embracing ugliness would require a blithe acceptance of mortality. Fat chance. However futile it feels, however much I want to aim for something fearsome and greater, I still turn my face to a flattering angle when the cameras come out.

Ugliness isn't something I've perfected, but it is, now, something I aspire to: something greater than beauty, and more achievable, since I write the rules myself. It is an action I can take, when I have the courage; I don't always have the courage, but the potential is there, a muscle I know I can learn how to flex if I try. I still look at successful artists who are very beautiful and think, *What I could do if I looked like her.* But I also do most of my best writing when I take definitive, deliberate steps away from acceptable feminine beauty. For many years, I had half my head shaved—not a deeply transgressive look in the grand scheme of things but challenging from a fat woman, who is supposed to keep curtains of hair to hide behind. (People could now see my double chin *quite clearly*, at least from the left!) And I know it wasn't just the haircut—some kind of reverse Samson thing—but it can't be denied that at around the same time, I started doing the kind of writing that got noticed. Maybe freeing myself from one of the trappings of femininity also acted as a release valve in other ways—or maybe, having done something people might stare at, I felt empowered to expect their attention, even to insist on it. Beauty may be a key, but a key is not the only way to open a door; you can do it with a battering ram. Ugliness lets me demand what may be given to the beautiful without a fight.

I don't always have the guts to be a Gorgon, but I can wear her on my breastplate: a talisman against the forces that want me to winnow myself away. When you embrace imperfection, your own imperfection stops consuming you. When your own imperfection stops consuming you, the imperfection itself can be art.

Whatever our monstrous new heroine looks like, whatever armor she wears, she too will carry the Gorgon's head on her shield. Ugliness for protection, and for bravery, and for defense. Ugliness for visibility, for forcing people to meet your eyes, for making them freeze and shiver when they do. Ugliness for an infinity of options, a universe unconstrained by any desire except your own.

VORACIOUS

HERE IS HOW MY ex-husband proposed to me: He didn't. Here is how I proposed: I don't know. I am pretty sure getting married was my idea, and I think that at first he didn't want to and then after a while he didn't not want to. Then we made plans. That's all.

But that's the way I wanted it. That's the kind of couple we were. On Valentine's Day, we would get a box of candy and split it; what was the point of buying two? I would have been mortified by flowers or love notes or public displays of affection. A boy with a crush had written me sonnets in grad school once, good sonnets that he printed in an Elizabethan font with the long S and everything. I had been a little flattered but also flustered and horrified and repulsed. I did not want, or need, to be told that I was lovable, that I was desirable, that I was pretty. I couldn't imagine wishing for such things, and I certainly couldn't imagine asking for them. The idea of someone devoting time, attention, energy, or money to making me happy made me profoundly uncomfortable.

I joked, for years, that I was "allergic to romance." What I really recoiled from, though, was the idea that romance might be something I would want. The wanting itself was a source of terror, something to be partitioned away and ignored. I wouldn't have minded being proposed to. But I certainly would have minded being the kind of girl who wouldn't mind.

☙

Not every monster devours, but the drive to consume—to gobble up children, or swallow the sun, or eat young women's hearts—is considered a monstrous trait. Outsize hunger is the province of the monster, and for women, all hungers are outsize. For a person who has learned to make herself physically and emotionally small, to live literally and figuratively on scraps, admitting to any appetite at all is admitting to monstrous gluttony. Women are often on a diet of the body, but we are always on a diet of the heart.

The low-maintenance woman, the ideal woman, has no appetite. This is not to say that she refuses food, sex, romance, emotional effort; to refuse is petulant, which is ironically more demanding. The woman without appetite politely finishes what's on her plate, and declines seconds. She is satisfied and satisfiable.

A man's appetite can be hearty, but a woman with an appetite is always voracious: her hunger always overreaches, because it is not supposed to exist. If she wants food, she is a glutton. If she wants sex, she is a slut. If she wants emotional caretaking, she is a high-maintenance bitch—or, worse, an "attention whore": an amalgam of sex-hunger and care-hunger, greedy not only to be fucked and paid but, most unforgivably of all, to be noticed.

"In the past couple of years, the 'attention-seeking' label has become an all-purpose way to gaslight feminists, silence those who demand restitution for a specific wrong, and shame women for the way they present their bodies and selves in public," writes Rebecca Onion in a *Slate* article unpacking the misogynist insult "She just wants attention." But underlying the attention-seeker's supposed sin is the eminently reasonable craving to be seen, considered, and taken seriously. "The desire to be known—to be paid mind—is profoundly human," Onion writes. It becomes "whorish" (itself a word designed to shame sex workers and concupiscent women) only in a context where any hunger, no matter how mundane, is considered outrageous.

The attention whore is every low-maintenance woman's dark mirror: the void of hunger we fear is hiding beneath our calculated restraint. It doesn't take much to be considered an attention whore. Any manifestation of that deeply natural need to be noticed and attended to is enough.

You don't have to be secretly needy to worry. You just have to be secretly human.

As a child, on an endless restrictive regimen that started when I was four, I was told, "If you get used to eating less, you'll stop being so hungry." The secret to satiation, to satisfaction, was not to meet or even acknowledge your needs but to curtail them. We learn the same lesson about our emotional hunger: Want less, and you will always have enough.

꩜

The enchantress Circe knows all about the risks of thoughtless consumption. When she's introduced in Homer's *Odyssey*, she turns Odysseus's crew into pigs after they gorge themselves on the drugged food she offers them. It's one of the few times that men, in myth, are punished for their appetites—and naturally, it's the work of an unnatural woman. It's also only the anonymous shipmen who fall for Circe's deceit; Odysseus himself is too crafty for the enchantress, too remarkable a hero to be kneecapped by his greed. After he rescues his men, he takes Circe to bed, and then remains on her island for a full year, feasting and fucking.

But once it's time for him to leave, Circe warns him again about the danger of hunger. His route, she tells him, will lead between two hazards: fearsome Scylla, who darts out six toothy heads to snatch six men from every ship that passes, and the even more terrible Charybdis, the implacable maelstrom, who sucks down water ravenously enough to destroy any craft.

In modern-day parlance, when we talk about navigating between Scylla and Charybdis, we mean doing a tricky tightrope walk to avoid two disastrous outcomes. But Circe's advice is unambiguous: Hug the Scylla side, and take your losses. It's better to sacrifice six of your men to a beast than to lose your whole crew to the vortex. If you must choose, even a vicious woman is better than a hungry one.

Charybdis is a whirlpool, a force of nature, but—like hurricanes of old—an unambiguously female one. Anthropologist David Gilmore describes her as "a voracious, man-eating female sea monster, a watery virago." In Servius's commentary on Virgil's *Aeneid*, he tells the story of Charybdis's origins. She was a voracious woman who was cast into the sea by Zeus as a punishment for stealing Heracles's cattle. (It's not specified whether she proposed to eat them, but it seems safe to assume.) There, she retains her original voracious nature by continuing to swallow everything.

That word "voracious" comes up over and over again to describe Charybdis. She is not only hungry. She is fueled by hunger, defined by it, driven by it. This is what makes her terrible—more terrible than Scylla, who will consume men, but only in known quantities. Charybdis's hunger is bottomless.

Charybdis, says Gilmore, "represents an archetypal dream image: that of losing control, being powerless, falling prey to powers beyond natural control." He's talking about men's fear, Odysseus's fear. But how much more terrifying must her boundless appetite be to Charybdis herself? She's been banished, punished, cast into the sea, but she can't stop feeding. Charybdis is a cautionary tale, not only to sailors, but to women: hunger destroys those around you. Hunger destroys control.

❧

Do I even have to tell you that I had a weird relationship to food when I was young? I'm female, Western, privileged, and a medium amount fat. Of course I did. I was never in danger of being diagnosed with any kind of eating disorder; at the time, it was a brand-new idea that people could even *have* an eating disorder if their weight wasn't dangerously low. But I threw up a lot, and skipped some meals, and frequently avoided eating in public, and mainlined junk food in private, and had all kinds of crypto-diet food weirdnesses that I filed under "picky eating." I simply didn't *like* avocados, or fish, or condiments, or spicy food, or any food with more than three components.

The primary effect was that I lost the ability to tell when I was hungry. Having yoked the act of eating—or not eating—to things like social standing and personal worth, I had unlinked it from the needs of my actual body. I didn't know how to recognize that I needed to eat, or make the necessary provisions. Sometimes I wouldn't realize it until the point of meltdown. More than once, I spent months plagued by mysterious stomach pains that turned out to have been hunger pangs.

Rediscovering hunger took concerted effort—effort that, honestly, still only works when I'm concentrating. When I'm not, I'll frequently leave out eating for most of the day, then make myself sick because my disastrously belated lunchtime runs up too close to my socially mandated dinner. Sometimes, hunger doesn't even kick in until someone puts food in front of me. I will rely on any other cue—the ease or difficulty of procuring food, the time of day, what other people are doing, the timing of my work and gym and social plans—before I'll remember to look inward. Imagine being told that your biggest secret—your weirdest sexual fantasy, your most embarrassing faceplant, your favorite Nickelback song—was supposed to dictate your behavior, publicly, as many as three times a day.

People frequently claim that eating disorders, like anything common to adolescent girls, are just "a cry for attention." As someone who was once an adolescent girl, I suspect they are at least partially the opposite: a cry against hunger and need, an attempt to kick away that profoundly human desire to be paid mind. To shut the door on the void.

Fearing hunger, fearing the loss of control that tips hunger into voraciousness, means fearing asking for anything: nourishment, attention, kindness, consideration, respect. Love, of course, and the manifestations of love. It means being so unwilling to seem "high-maintenance" that we pretend we do not need to be maintained. And eventually, it means losing the ability to recognize what it takes to maintain a self, a heart, a life.

So when I said, "I don't like romance," it was the equivalent of a dieter insisting she just doesn't *want* dessert. I did want it—I just thought I wasn't allowed.

❧

Any desire can become voracious, if it's forbidden. Take sex. The male sexual appetite is considered normal, an excuse even. Boys will be boys, who will want what they want. When a woman wants, we avert our eyes. It's a nakedness worse than nakedness, to be caught wanting.

I spent four years with a man who wouldn't fuck me. It's hard to talk about, not least because we were in fact having sex, an activity that you may be shocked to learn does not require both a penis and a vagina and the interaction of the two. (He *might* actually have been shocked to learn this. He was operating with a very hetero and, if you will, pre-Clinton-era idea of what "counts.") But there was a hard line, pun not intended. At first, this was his way of telling a self-protective story; I was an undergraduate in his class, but as long as we didn't do anything that *he* considered sex, he was exploiting nobody, breaking no rules, doing nothing wrong. Pretty quickly, though, it became a way of exerting dominance. Whatever he might have wanted out of me—and he was still getting plenty—was no match for the thrill of refusing me something. And maybe there was something too intimate, for him, about going any further; too revealing, too vulnerable. That's the sense I got. What I wanted, more than sex, was to be acknowledged; what he wanted, more than sex, was not to acknowledge me.

Because we were sleeping together (according to any reasonable definition) and also not sleeping together (according to him, and also, let's be real, compared to what I wanted to be doing), it's always been hard to express why this messed me up so much. It's not accurate to say he withheld sex, or denied me sex—except that it is. He clearly took a spiteful pleasure in limiting our interactions so that I never felt satisfied, and he never felt out of control. It's not accurate to say he used me for sex either, since that phrase when applied to a heterosexual relationship implies a whole wealth of things we didn't do. Except that, again, it is: He trusted that my infatuation would keep me available for whatever he did happen to want when he wanted it, *and* available to suffer entertainingly when he didn't want anything else. My desire became a leash to choke me with.

What this does to you, over time, is to slowly peel away your ability to express or even acknowledge that appetite. It's a cruelly inverted kind of sexual trauma, one that casts you as the offender, the architect of your own pain for wanting too much. Instead of the imposition of someone else's attention, what you fear is what bubbles up from your own core. The whirlpool. The vortex.

Sexual denial is, perhaps, even harder to wrap your head around than hunger—because women aren't just supposed to lack these urges, we're also supposed to acquiesce to having them imposed upon us by others. How much more complicated would our relationship to food be if it were still outrageous to express hunger, but *also* embarrassingly Puritan to resist being force-fed? But it's all of a piece: the yearning for attention, the yearning for sex, the yearning to have what you want when you want it and not be subjected to judgment on whether it's deserved. The yearning to operate outside of that judgment: to transcend deserving, or at least to unhook deserving from desire. To be allowed to want what you may not be granted. To want it anyway, without shame.

⌒

I believe there are people who truly dislike romantic gestures, in the same way there are people who truly dislike sweets. And it's certainly true that a lot of what passes for "romance" in our broad cultural definition—the Jumbotron proposal, the bed covered in rose petals—has been neatly split from genuine emotion, like a painted eggshell blown clear of its guts. It's a charade of romance, a mask we give straight men to wear when they're frightened or confused by showing their naked face. I truly did not want that, and I still don't, and I never will. Being dragooned into acting as a partner in these romantic pageants is like having one of those dreams where you're hauled up on stage unprepared.

But attentiveness, consideration, compliments, small and large kindnesses, feeling truly loved, having someone put you first while you put them first because you're in cahoots to make each other's lives easier and better: most people do like that, when it's thoughtful and sincere. It's here, more than in the big gestures, that romance lives: in being actively caring and thoughtful, in a way that is reciprocal but not transactional.

And yet, for most of my life, I never would have asked for or expected such a thing. Many women wouldn't, even the ones who secretly or not-so-secretly pine to be treated like a princess. It's one thing to fantasize about a perfect proposal or an expensive gift; that's high-maintenance, sure, but it's also par for the course. It's asking something from a man, but primarily it's asking him to step into an already choreographed mating dance—a mannered two-step from the days of courtly love, when it was the woman's job to stand on a pedestal whether she liked it or not, and the man's job to write sonnets about her eyebrows. That was the predominant expression of love at a pivotal time in Western culture; a man doesn't have to have read Spenser's sonnets to be familiar with and comfortable in that mode. But asking to be thought of, understood, prioritized: this is a request so deep it is almost unfathomable. It's a voracious request, a monstrous request, the demand of the attention whore.

Women talk ourselves into needing less, because we're not supposed to want more—or because we know we won't get more, and we don't want to feel unsatisfied. We reduce our needs for food, for space, for respect, for help, for love and affection, for touch, for being noticed, according to what we think we're allowed to have. Sometimes we tell ourselves that we can live without it, even that we don't want it. But it's not that we don't want more. It's that we don't want to be seen asking for it. And when it comes to romance, women always, always need to ask.

❧

There's a YouTube video I'm fond of that shows a baby named Madison being given cake for the first time. The maniacal shine in her eyes when she first tastes chocolate icing is transcendent, a combination of "Where has this been all my life?" and "How dare you keep this from me?" Jaw still dropped in shock, she slowly tips the cake up towards her face and plunges in, mouth first. Periodically, as she comes up for air, she shoots the camera a look that is almost anguished. *Can you believe this exists?* her face says. *Why can't I get it all in my mouth at once?*

This video makes me laugh uproariously, but it's that throat-full-of-needles laugh that, on a more hormonal day, might be a sob. The raw, unashamed carnality of this baby going to town on a cake is like a glimpse into a better, hungrier world. This may be one of the last times Madison is allowed to express that kind of appetite, that kind of greed. She's still young enough for it to be cute.

This is Madison's first birthday. By the time she's ten, there's an 80 percent chance she'll have been on a diet. By high school, she's likely to have shied away from expressing public opinions; she'll speak up less in class, bite back objections and frustrations, shrug more, stay silent, look at the ground. She'll worry about seeming "good"—which means not too pushy, not too demanding, not too loud. (Only spoiled girls want better. Only sluts want more.) Boys will treat her shoddily, and she will find ways to shrink herself into the cracks they leave for her. She will learn to assert less, to demand less, to desire less. She won't grab for anything with both hands; she won't tip anything towards her face and plunge in. And that transcendent anguish, that stark gluttony . . . well, at least we'll have it caught on video.

Imagine being Madison, grown up but undimmed. Imagine being a woman who is unabashed about needing food to survive and pleasure to be fulfilled and care to be happy. Imagine unleashing the whirlpool of your hunger, and letting it consume indiscriminately, and realizing the world is not destroyed.

We are told that Charybdis claimed countless ships in her everlasting greed. But the best made it through: Odysseus, Jason, Aeneas (all of them protected by goddesses, natch). The heroes, the worthies, everyone whose story gets told. Maybe it's only the fragile who fall before women's hunger. Maybe the hunger itself is nothing to fear.

And Charybdis herself, unlike so many other monsters, was never defeated. That in itself is something to wonder at: that female voraciousness is so fearsome that it can only be avoided, never fought. How do you even fight hunger? You can't punch it, you can't stab it, you can't cut off its heads. You can ignore it, belittle it, make it seem shameful and insignificant—but it will still be there, a small angry vortex, waiting. Heroes have survived Charybdis, but they've never had the best of her.

❦

What helped for me is that I became adored. This was extremely unfamiliar; I'd always been the one doing the work of adoring, if there was any adoring being done, which is as exhausting as taking on any other solo emotional burden. I have had entire partnerships, long ones, fueled, I realized later, by pure relief at my own indifference. When you've burned out all your circuits adoring someone for nothing, getting to be indifferent feels like grace.

Adoration certainly wasn't something that existed in my marriage—although really, whose fault was that? Being too low-maintenance, carving yourself hollow to make space for someone who never asked you to, is not actually a generous way to live. You become so obsessed with giving ground that you forget to show up—you're just a walking, talking "I dunno, what do *you* want to do?" Don't get me wrong: I've known men who would see me curled up small on the extreme margin of the relationship and complain that I was breathing too loud. But once you get settled in there, clinging to the edge, you can't really blame a trusting person for assuming that's the space you need. Possibly I wasn't adored in my previous partnerships because I was barely there at all.

My first experience being adored was with someone who didn't actually know me very well. I was freshly out of a marriage that had been companionable but not fulfilling, and he was desperate to have some kind of connection and commitment, with anyone. For once, I was the one staying aloof, and the other party was adoring with all his might. It's hard to say, now, how much I actually believed we were in love; the best I can do is "sort of, but not really, but sort of really." It became clear very quickly that we were not—that we were each in love with a bodiless something, to which we had given the other's face. Still, for a fragile moment, and for the first time in memory, I was adored. And contrary to expectation, I found I had a taste for the stuff. Being adored whether I wanted it or not—and in this case, I decided pretty early on that I didn't—did a curious thing for me. It made me feel important. As important, even, as a man. Instead of expecting me to downplay my hungers, there was someone trying to fill up my plate. I'm sure it doesn't work this way for everyone, but for me, having someone treat me with care—after decades of professing that I didn't even want to be cared for—showed up my dislike of romance for the self-protective fiction it was. It felt impossible to start pushing the plate away again.

When my now-husband and I had been dating for a month, he sent me a pie. He'd accompanied his family on vacation to Key West, Florida, and texted me many pictures of polydactyl cats and chickens and cocktails and key lime pie. I was in bed with the flu, and found this vicarious vacation sustaining, especially coming from him. The fact that he dubbed one particularly daunting dessert "Mt. Keylimeanjaro" helped cement my sense that this was the guy for me. On his last day, he texted me: "Would you be freaked out if I got you a souvenir from Key West?" "Ooooh," I said, "is it pie?" I thought I was joking. Shortly after he got home a key lime pie arrived at my apartment, packed in dry ice.

"I feel like I *should* be creeped out, in a way?" I wrote to a friend. "Because we are strenuously trying not to do anything serious, but also we talk all the time and he sent me a pie." In general, I was worried—or, more accurately, worried that I should worry—that he was more into me than I was into him, a situation that would have been extremely unfamiliar and therefore frightening. He seemed too attentive, too affectionate, too committal in action even though we both staunchly maintained our independence in words. Who sends a whole pie just to say "thinking of you"?

And yet—though I've never sent a pie, I have picked up treats, knitted scarves, left notes, made presents, bought shirts, texted to check in, done chores that weren't mine because I didn't mind making somebody else's life easier. When you're raised as a woman you're trained in this kind of happy servitude, and I happened to take to it. It just hadn't occurred to me to expect, or even accept, the same in return. If asked, I would have said I didn't want it. Expecting it, even wanting it, always felt like an act of monstrous greed.

What if I decided I did want it, though? What if it turned out I liked pie, and kindness, and having other people think of me as much as I thought of them?

Sometimes, it's only when somebody puts food in front of you that you realize you were hungry after all.

❧

Women who are unlucky enough to love men are working at two disadvantages: we are expected to do things for them, and they are expected to sit back and let things be done. Just as keeping one's appetite in check is treated as a standard part of femininity, lack of sentiment is baked into our concept of what it means to be a man. The masculine guy lights out for the territories, alone with his horse, who doesn't have a birthday. Tracking milestones, buying gifts, maintaining friendships, anticipating wants and needs: these are the province of women, not his concern.

My husband keeps a dossier on his phone of basic information about me: birthday, family's names, favorite apple types and ice cream flavors, gift ideas, tampon brand in case I need him to pick some up. I don't know everything that's in it, though I've been told I can submit a FOIA request and allow two to four months for sensitive information to be redacted. (I do know that a lot of it is about food preferences; as someone trained to renounce hunger I am occasionally seized with embarrassment about this, and will even sometimes refuse to let him add more food opinions to the list.) The effort of keeping the dossier is minimal, only barely more onerous than taking a moment to note someone's likes and dislikes without writing them down. But when I tell people about it, they're generally floored. Men are assumed to be capable of tracking work deadlines, bills, stock performance, fantasy football stats. A friend recently sent me a picture of the fifty-line spreadsheet he uses to remember which shoes he prefers. Paying attention to details about your partner, though—that's bizarre.

Personally, I remember birthdays, family names, favorite foods, sometimes even social security numbers for every boyfriend I've ever had, and some men who never would have called themselves my "boyfriend." I happen to be good at holding such details in my mind forever, but it's not just that—it's the fact that I'm expected to pay attention. My husband is not, culturally, expected to pay attention. He could, and many men would, shrug and say "You know I'm not good at remembering these things." He's not, in fact, good at remembering them—but he recognizes their importance. Hence the dossier: an external tool to supplement his memory, like a to-do list or a calendar. The kind of tool we employ when something matters.

It was terrifying, at first, to realize that my husband wasn't just equitable—he was a natural caretaker, more at home providing effort than accepting it. He has an ingrained cordiality from being raised wealthy and Southern, but it goes beyond that (as a child, he wanted to grow up to be a butler). He'll always offer to get you something while he's up, but he's also more than happy to get up if you need something. For a long time, I thought of this solicitousness as a sort of fault line. If I pushed it too hard, surely everything would fall apart, not only our relationship but our lives. Here was someone willing to pay attention to my needs, to anticipate them, even—but I had no idea how much need I was truly capable of. Would coddling just invite me to ask for more? Would I find that denying my desire to be cared for was the only thing keeping that hunger under control? I envisioned turning into a sort of overfed queen bee, luxuriating in adoration, unwilling to do basic chores or leave the apartment or do much besides signal from the couch for another drink.

In the mid-1940s, researchers at the University of Minnesota had volunteers drastically reduce their caloric intake for six months, and studied the effects of their physical and mental health. The Minnesota Starvation Experiment, as it's known, could never be replicated today—human subject regulations wouldn't allow a repeat of such a patently inhumane study. But it has formed the basis for a great deal of scientific knowledge about what happens to humans when they can't get enough food for weeks or months at a time.

One of the things we know for a fact because of this study is also something we could probably have intuited: starving people, given access to food, will often eat until they're ill. The study's authors described what happened after the diet ended: "Subject No. 20 stuffs himself until he is bursting at the seams, to the point of being nearly sick and still feels hungry; No. 120 reported that he had to discipline himself to keep from eating so much as to become ill; No. 1 ate until he was uncomfortably full; and subject No. 30 had so little control over the mechanics of 'piling it in' that he simply had to stay away from food because he could not find a point of satiation even when he was 'full to the gills.'" Even after months and months back on a normal diet, some subjects were still regularly eating until they couldn't eat anymore.

Eventually, though, the starved men began to eat normally again. Their hunger, once seemingly implacable, leveled off. They learned what they'd forgotten in their months of privation: It is possible to be full.

The fear of expressing hunger, of any kind, is in part a fear of finding that hunger to be bottomless. Bottomless hunger consumes you, turns you into a void, a whirlpool, a ravening mouth. But in the end, nothing makes you hungrier than starving. It's not indulgence that brings on bottomless hunger—it's denial.

❧

Here is how my husband proposed: He brought me breakfast.

It was the last day of 2017, the final day of the deadline he'd given himself: *this year.* I was lying in bed in our borrowed apartment in Berlin, wondering how to deal with the fact that his time was up. We'd been on vacation for a week, including any number of romantic opportunities—an opera singer busking under a full moon by the Berlinerdom, a perfect secret cocktail bar in Kreuzberg—and now it was the last day of our trip and the last day of the year. I hadn't asked for a time frame, but he'd offered one, and what was I supposed to do if he didn't come through? And then he called me into the living room, where he had coffee and pastries from the shop downstairs, like all the other mornings of our trip, and a sheaf of roses he'd walked all over to find because it was a holiday, and a family ring he'd flown down to his parents' to get even though he knew it was far too much ring for me to actually wear. New Year's Eve in Berlin is a riot of fireworks, progressing throughout the day from an unnerving but distant rumble to a festive war zone. We sat in our temporary living room and listened to the first explosions start.

I may not have asked for a time frame, but I *had* asked for a proposal. When we first decided to get married, I told him, "I've been married before, but I've never been proposed to, so can you arrange that?" He said yes, of course. (He's a Southern boy and was going to do it anyway.) Then he fretted and dallied about it for so long I almost regretted asking. It felt important, though, to insist on this, an act of adoration beyond anything I would have been able to accept ten years before. It felt important for it to be his responsibility entirely, not because of a patriarchal tradition I didn't care about but because of a new, proudly monstrous appetite for affection I very much did.

I know how it sounds, to stipulate that someone not only agree to link their life to yours but petition you, *implore* you for the privilege. I was brought up thinking that my love would be something people acquiesced to, or did not; certainly commitment, at least commitment to me, was never going to be *aspirational*. That's how it played out in my first marriage: I suggested, and he agreed, with the degree of ambivalence that I had been led to expect. And yet here I was demanding, in effect, a formal application for being allowed to spend a lifetime with me. As though that was a prize!

Only a few years earlier, this request would have seemed voracious, avaricious, absolutely disconnected from both logic and economics. How could I overvalue my own worth to the point where I thought I could require this level of effort? But there are other kinds of hunger too. There's the kind that yawns indiscriminately and sucks the whole world down—and there's the kind that lends savor to a good meal, a hunger you can enjoy because it is well-earned and satisfiable. You can't recognize the difference if you've never been less than starved.

࿔

Charybdis, the whirlpool, is in real life probably a system of tidal disturbances in the Strait of Messina, off Sicily. She's surprisingly tame, for a mythic monster—a danger to small crafts, maybe, but nothing of note. On YouTube, you can watch a forty-nine-year-old man swim across the strait, though it's very dull. Spoiler: he isn't consumed.

Charybdis, the monster, mythologizes these unpredictable eddies into a ravenous void. A little embellishment, a smattering of fear, and a choppy strait becomes an impassable gateway. A request to be seen, to be thought of, becomes an act of gluttony. A woman becomes a hazard, or a beast.

You can't punch hunger. You can't stab it. You can't cut off its heads. All you can do is feed it, and in feeding it, realize that it is not insatiable. The fear of voraciousness is mythic, but the hunger itself is nothing to fear. As a trait, in fact, hunger is heroic. This is true in a literal sense: when Odysseus leaves Circe's island with her instructions on avoiding Charybdis, he has been gorging on her food for a solid year. But more than that, hunger means a drive to do more, to have more, and the energy to make that drive real. Denying us our hunger is part of how they've kept us from heroism for so long.

But hunger comes back with a vengeance, when you let it, when it's freed. The hunger for food rushes back, and behind it, the hunger for love, for attention, for achievement, for victory. In *The Odyssey*, Odysseus doesn't defeat Charybdis, but more than that, he almost loses to her. His boat wrecked by Zeus in punishment for a transgression, he is borne by the current back towards that gulping mouth; he survives only by clinging to a tree, holding himself aloft as the vortex sucks up his raft. In the story of Charybdis as the whirlpool would tell it, perhaps she triumphs—not as a monster destroying the hero, but as a hero herself, overwhelming and defeating a trespasser on behalf of the king of the gods. In this story, her voraciousness is her weapon and her gift. What strength the unapologetically hungry monster-heroine could have: enough to swallow a man.

DOGS BELOW
THE WAIST

ALL I DID IN VIENNA was eat cake and look at medical oddities. It's a wonderful city for the history of medicine, a field I've been drawn to since college—and in particular, it's a wonderful city for my preferred interaction with the history of medicine, which involves less learning dates and more looking at slightly gruesome displays in haunted-looking museums and cluttered Wunderkammers. Vienna's museums specialize in wax moulage. The rooms that circle the Narrenturm, the ring-shaped building that houses the Museum of Pathological Anatomy, are adorned with lovingly crafted wax faces, buttocks, and genitals, each peeking from a cradle of pinstriped cloth, each crusted or warted or eaten away with disease. The history of medicine museum at the University of Vienna's medical school, known as the Josephinum, features rows of wax bones in cases, severed legs with veins made of wax-dipped thread, and full fleshless bodies standing in upright glass boxes as though you've caught them in the shower. It's like a cross between Madame Tussauds and an abattoir.

In the middle of one of the rooms of the Josephinum, laid out in a glass coffin like Snow White, is the figure of a beautiful nude woman. She lies on her back, in a pose suggesting intoxication or orgasm more than sleep: one knee slightly bent, hands rucking the silk sheets beneath her, her head tilted back in abandon or ecstasy. She has been slashed open from throat to groin. Her breasts hang to the sides, just flaps of wax, and her guts are a bulbous dark mass against her alabaster skin, coils of intestine resting on a pristine hip. On top of her long blonde hair, which spills prettily around her shoulders, is a delicate circlet of gold.

Next to her, in a similar glass and rosewood box, lies another lounging blonde figure, this one wearing a string of pearls. Her torso, too, is open, but not in the manner of a crime or an autopsy. The front of her torso has simply been sliced off in a neat, bloodless curve and deposited elsewhere. Instead of breasts, she has smooth expanses of light brown lung underneath her pearls. Under that, her diaphragm folds like a wing over her stomach and a neat tongue of pancreas. Something, maybe a kidney, lies by her side. Her eyes are open, and her expression is not exactly orgasmic; it is, more than anything, resigned. Tucked inside her pelvis is a fetus the size of a fist.

These are "anatomical Venuses," an eighteenth–century innovation in medical display: lovingly detailed wax models of ideal feminine beauties, with real eyelashes and human hair and jewelry and abdomens full of gore. The Josephinum Venuses, and a number of other surviving Venuses of Europe, come out of the wax workshop of a Florentine museum: the Museum for Physics and Natural History, also known as La Specola. La Specola, like the Josephinum, is full of models depicting aspects of human anatomy—"an encyclopedia of the human body in wax," as Joanna Ebenstein puts it in her lavishly photographed book *The Anatomical Venus*. Unlike dissection, wax was sanitary, odorless, and stable over a long period of time. It was also, potentially, beautiful. Wax models could be rendered placid and pain-free, their otherwise lovely faces and bodies drawing the mind away from death and towards higher (and lower) things. Like the Renaissance anatomical illustrations that preceded them, the La Specola waxworks were intended to show the hand of God in the human design. The luminous wax sculptures even called to mind earlier religious figurines. But they were also meant to be visually, even sexually, appealing. (This is why, despite the preponderance of male anatomical illustrations and models and cadaver dissections, there was no male equivalent of the Venus.) Ebenstein quotes eighteenth-century anatomical illustrator Arnaud-Éloi Gautier d'Agoty: "For men to be instructed, they must be seduced by aesthetics, but how can anyone render the image of death agreeable?" The anatomical Venus was the answer: the instructional realism of human innards, leavened by the seductive aesthetics of feminine beauty.

But to the modern eye, there's something uncanny, even upsetting about this image. If the Venus continues to fascinate, it is because she makes manifest something we'd rather ignore: Behind every perfect face and breast is a horrible jumble of meat. Our culture's relentless obsession with female bodies extends only as far as the skin; we're all supposed to covet the ideal female form as an image or a possession but not as an actual carcass. Once the lid of the torso lifts off, we shudder and turn away. Even the ubiquitous images of stylized violence against women, which echo the Venus in their juxtaposition of beauty and gore, are intended to position the body as a pristine canvas on which passion is enacted—sexual passion or violent passion, but anyway, the passion of a man. The beautiful corpses of television still don't void their bowels. What the anatomical Venus highlights, and what we now choose to ignore, is not violence but the gross corporeality of even the loveliest human body, the thin line separating the trophy from the cadaver. At the height of the age of the Venus, this was considered instructive, but now we mostly find it offensive. Ebenstein's book also quotes the British *Literary Gazette* from 1825 about an anatomical Venus display: "It is a large, disgusting doll, the alvus of which being taken off like a pot-lid, shows the internal parts, heart, liver, lungs, kidney, &c. . . . The thing is a silly imposture, and as indecent as it is wretched." "Indecent" sums up how many people feel about women's embodiment. Contemplating how this object of desire is also full of farts, sweat, germs, and pee is like picking up a Fabergé egg and realizing it's been packed with rotting meat.

In other words, if you are seen as feminine and have a mortal body, you are born monster.

❧

To Homer, writing in the eighth century BCE, Scylla was a twelve-legged, six-headed, barking creature with no human characteristics to speak of. As described in *The Odyssey*, she lives in a clifftop cave across from the whirlpool of Charybdis, with her twelve horrible feet hanging horribly down. When ships go by, she darts out her hideous heads, each one armed with several rows of teeth, and snatches men from the decks to eat, six at a time. The cave opening is very far up the cliff—the witch Circe, who warns Odysseus about Scylla, tells him that an arrow shot from a ship passing below wouldn't reach that far. In other words, Scylla's necks are *upsettingly* long. Odysseus never quite gets a glimpse of her, but he does see the legs and feet of the crewmen she scoops up, dangling over his head. Twelve legs hanging down.

By the time Ovid came around, though, seven hundred or so years later, Scylla's terrifying heads had migrated below the waist. His version of the story starts with Scylla as a nymph, the unwitting (or just uninterested) crush object of a sea god named Glaucus, who himself had recently been transformed from a mortal. Glaucus appeals to Circe for help in catching Scylla's eye, and Circe says, "I'll do you one better: Forget about her and you can have me instead." This does not have the intended effect. Instead of dropping the indifferent nymph for a demigod enchantress who's good to go—clearly the logical decision based on economic factors, but the heart wants what it wants—Glaucus declares that his love for Scylla will never change. So a jealous Circe decides to change Scylla instead. She laces the pool Scylla bathes in with herbs that cause a horrifying metamorphosis. As she wades into the water up to her waist, Scylla finds her legs and groin transformed into a mass of barking dogs.

The real moment of horror in Ovid's version of the story, the detail that makes it stick with you more than the ones where boys turn into flowers and girls into trees, is that when Scylla first looks down and sees herself surrounded by wild dogs, she tries to run. I'll quote it, because the moment is chilling and the translator (Rolfe Humphries) is fun:

> There Scylla came; she waded into the water,
> Waist-deep, and suddenly saw her loins disfigured
> With barking monsters, and at first she could not
> Believe that these were parts of her own body.
> She tried to drive them off, the barking creatures,

And flees in panic, but what she runs away from
She still takes with her; feeling for her thighs,
Her legs, her feet, she finds, in all these parts,
The heads of dogs, jaws gaping wide, and hellish.
She stands on dogs gone mad, and loins and belly
Are circled by those monstrous forms.

The monstrousness doesn't come solely from Scylla's new shape. (Personally, I wouldn't mind being partially dogs.) What inspires fear in this story is the sheer alienness of her body, now so unfamiliar that she wants to flee. What inspires true horror is the fact that she can't.

Or at least, that's what inspires horror to *me*. To the male poets and chroniclers telling Scylla's story, the horror is in the contrast between her beautiful face and her monstrous nethers. This isn't just a parable about embodiment, but about female embodiment, and the revulsion and confusion it often engenders in men. After all, Scylla doesn't turn *completely* into dogs. Virgil's *Aeneid*, from around the same time period as Ovid, is pretty straightforward about where the shift occurs: "Her upper parts are human; / down to the pubes she seems a lovely-breasted / virgin; but underneath she is a monster / come from the sea, a terrifying body." This is the same thing Shakespeare's King Lear is talking about when he says of women, "But to the girdle do the gods inherit / Beneath is all the fiend's."

Lear is specifically talking about vaginas—"There's hell, there's darkness, there's the sulfurous pit," okay, buddy, we get it—but this fear attaches to any woman's genitals (though trans women have to contend with a whole other set of people's fears). The issue isn't anything specific to the genitals themselves, but inherent to genitalia as a class: they have a smell and taste, they sport hair, they are associated with excretion. The genitals are a distillation of everything earthy and mammalian about bodies, everything that makes women into mammals instead of objects or angels, slapped down right where the ultimate prize is supposed to be. The male-gaze establishment sees sex with women as something to be won— the primary purpose of women, and one of the primary goals of men. And yet, standing in the way of this goal is the inconveniently corporeal nature of the bodies one is presumably having sex with. The disgust and horror stem not from the bodies per se but from the gulf between reality and fantasy.

When we talk about women's bodies being turned into sexual objects, we don't always note that these objects have little to do with the bodies themselves. Bodies that are objectified in the literal sense—reproduced as sex toys or perfume bottles or novelty cigarette lighters or decor at the Korova Milk Bar—are rendered as impossibly smooth, tucked, monochrome (almost always in shades of white). Women's bodies that are externally commodified, in porn made by and for men but also in advertising and acting and modeling, are expected to be kept as free of hair and lines and folds as possible, regardless of effort and expense; photo editing does the rest. The actual woman's body—genitals especially, but really all the less-sanitized aspects of embodiment that the genitals represent—is something you tolerate because, essentially, we live in a fallen world. Women's real-life bodies are the shadow on the cave wall, the debased reflection of something purer and more precious.

❧

Like a lot of young women, I was an occasional self-harmer in my teens and twenties. This is usually understood either to be a cry for attention or a form of stress relief, and both were a little true in my case, although it was more accurately a cry for tenderness. I have always been easily overwhelmed, and a sharp and controlled sensation helps focus the mind. I have also never felt that I deserved to be treated kindly unless I tricked somebody into pity (which, counterproductively, I would usually then reject). But much more than either of those factors, cutting was a way to signal my rejection of my body. It was a kind of ritual, a microcosmic imitation of something I wanted to invoke on a grand scale.

I thought often, during this time, of the scene in C. S. Lewis's *The Voyage of the Dawn Treader* in which obnoxious Eustace is turned into a dragon. Like the metamorphosis of Scylla, it's a moment of true body horror: Eustace, waking up transformed, at first thinks he's lying between two dragons, because he can see scaly arms on either side of him. He scrambles to get away, but the arms move with him. Eventually, he realizes he is trapped in a dragon body himself, and that his terrifying exterior will cut him off from humankind for good. With the help of Aslan, the lion Messiah of Narnia, he realizes that his dragon skin can be flaked off: "I started scratching myself and my scales began coming off all over the place. And then I scratched a little deeper and, instead of just scales coming off here and there, my whole skin started peeling off beautifully, like it does after an illness, or as if I was a banana. In a minute or two I just stepped out of it. I could see it lying there beside me, looking rather nasty. It was a most lovely feeling." But shallowly scratching off his dragon skin only reveals another, newer layer. It takes a divine intervention from Aslan to truly free him of his horrifying body: "The very first tear he made was so deep that I thought it had gone right into my heart. And when he began pulling the skin off, it hurt worse than anything I've ever felt. The only thing that made me able to bear it was just the pleasure of feeling the stuff peel off." He compares it to picking the scab off of a wound.

This moment was in the back of my mind when I did pick off scabs to reopen old cuts, or made new ones, or peeled skin off my hands and feet to the point of blood. These shallow scratches would never free me from the misshapen, mistaken body I'd been trapped in, the one that would make humans reject me and doom me to permanent loneliness—but maybe they could call down the lion's claw.

I knew Eustace's de-dragoning, like much in Narnia, was a religious metaphor, and therefore not really applicable to me—but then again, rejection of the body always smacks of religion. Starvation and self-mutilation have long been the purview of both teenage girls and saints. The saints, of course, think there's something more to them than the physical, thus rendering the body useless at best, at worst an anchor to the material realm. I've never thought that. I've always known that my mind was, as my husband once put it, "an epiphenomenon of a bunch of really weird meat." How do you long to be free of the body without believing in a soul? I suppose I thought there was a way to feel safe and comfortable and at ease in *a* body—it just hadn't ever been mine. What stepped out of Eustace's dragon hide was Eustace himself, back in a form he recognized, soft and smooth and made better by his ordeal. My wild, unspoken wish was that I might discover a body where I felt at home, if I could crack open my shell.

Needless to say, this did not happen. I've come to a kind of grudging acceptance of embodiment—and I've channeled my dragon-hide-removal instincts into minor casualties like pulling out my eyebrows or picking the skin off my thumbs—but I can't say I like it. What a flawed, unreliable, uncomfortable, and frequently maligned vehicle I have to carry my mind around in! What's even worse is the fact that it is, of course, not a vehicle at all—that my consciousness literally arises from this faulty, fleshy stuff. I'm not saying there aren't rewards to having a body. Obviously there are. I'm just saying there aren't any rewards that couldn't be adequately mimicked if I were a well-cared-for brain in a jar.

The whole body thing is, frankly, exhausting to me. It generally feels like more of a burdensome pet. I'm never quite sure I'm cleaning it right; it's like if someone handed you a horse and said "curry this," with no further explanation. After nearly forty years, you'd probably land on a decent solution for a minimally dirty horse, but you'd still have the nagging idea that you don't *really* know what "currying" is. Feeding it, especially if I'm tired or stressed in any way at all, is a source of immense frustration and ennui, and while I like food fine, I've never been able to work hard to optimize taste, variety, or nutrition. (My ideal food situation is something I don't especially like but don't hate and that is available without too much thinking; well-stocked grocery stores paralyze me.) With a few exceptions, I do not trust it to move me around in any but the most conventional ways. This is partly because I'm out of shape, but also partly *why* I am: When you can't rely on your body not to betray and humiliate you, it's hard to submit it to any exercise that will build endurance or strength.

The body is also sometimes a source of distress. I am frequently convinced that it's ill or infested in some way, particularly because I'm bad at filtering out sensory input, which means among other things that I am itchy *all the time.* Or maybe that's not the reason—I'm also laughably incompetent at understanding cause and effect when it comes to my own body, and can't really understand how other people make connections like "When I eat a certain food, I feel bad in a specific way." (This makes me immune to many addictions—I probably experience withdrawal symptoms, but I don't realize what they are—but also makes me faintly ridiculous a lot of the time. In my early twenties, when I lived with a boyfriend who made me cry all the time, I would constantly wake up in the morning with horribly puffy eyes, so I assumed I was having some kind of allergy attack.) Remember the early days of the COVID pandemic, when everyone was scared they had the virus, but then realized their chest hurt because they were hunched over their laptop on the couch, or they were flushed and lightheaded not from fever but from anxiety and anger, or their headache was due to stress-drinking? I did the same thing, but in my case, I'd also been doing it for the previous forty years. I never go to the doctor, though, because the only thing more embarrassing than having a body is having to admit that you have one.

This discomfort with my corporeal form isn't just about sex, but of course it's also about sex, one of the primary recreational things you can do with a body if so inclined. Shortly after I started having sex as a teen, penetration became irritating and painful. It turned out to be because of birth control pills, but I didn't figure this out for fifteen years, during which my ability to enjoy penetrative sex always dropped off precipitously as soon as I was having it regularly enough to bother getting a prescription. No doctors were especially concerned or especially interested in helping, so I assumed it was more or less usual. (Which, in a way, it was. In my experience and the experience of every woman I know, doctors who *are* concerned and interested in helping are much, much rarer than doctors who are so dismissive of female bodies—especially fat or, ironically, ill ones—that they are unable or unwilling to provide decent care. Even professional analysts of Down There Horror Dogs don't want to deal with the Down There Horror Dogs.) One gynecologist told me to use lube. Another told me with visible disgust that I probably had a yeast infection and handed me a tube of numbing cream and a prescription for an outrageously aggressive antifungal pill. Who knows what damage I did trying to repeatedly cure a yeast infection I didn't have? I certainly don't know. The only thing more embarrassing than admitting you have a body is paying it any kind of close attention.

My assumption is always that everyone will feel as put-upon by this body as I do. I'm mystified by friends, especially friends who aren't conventionally attractive, who are able to present their bodies as plausible objects of aesthetic or sexual value. If you can post a picture in your lingerie, or tell a cute person you just met that you want to go home with them, you might as well have told me you can fly.

This disconnect is so deep-seated and so lifelong that I have a hard time blaming it on societal expectations. It feels like something that was always there, or rather not there, in my brain, some unplugged cord left dangling. What I know, though, is that my attitude towards physicality has been cemented, for almost four decades, by countless confirming messages from the rest of the world. A few of those have been about my particular body, but much more significant, I think, is the way that revulsion towards women's bodies is just kind of in the air. It's such a prevalent trope that it almost feels facile to list examples. Take, for instance, the way so much of our culture still treats periods as a red-tent taboo, to the point that advertising for "feminine hygiene" products (they're period products!) displays blue fluid, and even unused tampons are hidden furtively as though they are borderline obscene. (This has human rights ramifications too. Activists have struggled to get free period supplies for imprisoned women, because lawmakers don't want to talk or think about periods.) Take the assumption that women will be thoroughly depilated in the few places we grudgingly admit they have hair—effortlessly depilated, mind you! Ladies take too long in the shower!—and the stubborn refusal to admit that they grow hair anywhere else. Take the cruel transphobic jokes, still considered acceptable enough to be mainstream, about what one might find under a woman's skirt. Take the animus towards fat female bodies, which is so corrosive that I've seen hateful, judgmental comments about sketches and cartoons. (Presumably you're worried about the drawing's "health"?) Take every single not-joking joke about how girls don't fart or sweat or defecate, or at least wouldn't dare do so in front of a man, or at least might realistically get dumped if they did.

This is only compounded if you have a chronic illness or disability, which may make it feel that the patriarchy *and* the general setup of literally everything in the world *and* sometimes your own body are all out to get you. My relationship with my body didn't have to be this adversarial—or rather, the one being adversarial in this relationship is me. Ill or disabled women face not only more antagonism from their actual bodies, but additional challenges from society: poor accommodations, sidelining, condescension, skepticism. Men love a fragile woman until she breaks.

To a certain degree, though, this is a difference of quantity rather than kind. The scorn heaped on ill and disabled people is (in part) capitalism writ large: If you are not productive, you are nothing. (As Esmé Weijun Wang writes in *Elle*, "My deep fear is that I'm secretly slothful and am using chronic illness to disguise the sick rot of laziness within myself. . . . Though it might be better to realize my worth outside of productivity, I continue to live in a society that praises the art of getting things done over all else—including wellness and rest—and these are values I can't seem to shake.") This only became more overt during the pandemic, as desperate capitalist profiteers became more and more explicit in saying that the economy matters more than the lives of the elderly or the ill. In the same way, the additional anger and judgment that disabled women, specifically, face about their bodies is influenced by the way women's bodies are generally maligned. Not just in the obvious ways—treated as vessels for lust or childbearing, and otherwise a failure—though there is that, of course. But there's more: illness, whether chronic or acute, underlines the basic *neediness* of the body, shows it up as the fumbling animal it is. The hallmarks of disease are the hallmarks of embodiment, in all its mundane grossness: vomiting, swelling, limping, leaking, all those perfectly human capacities women aren't supposed to admit to. Being sick, or getting sick—because disability can happen to anyone—means admitting that your body is not only fallible but *mammalian*, mucky and hairy and smelly and vulnerable, like anything else that crawls the earth. Pain and disease are brutally physical, actively resisting any attempt to transcend the flesh.

I do technically have at least one chronic illness: endometriosis, a relatively common condition in which the endometrium, which normally lines the uterus, goes feral and starts growing wherever it wants. It's never exactly absent—I am always a little aware of my ovaries, the way you're aware of a person standing just behind you—but it also hasn't seriously hampered my life since I had surgery for it when I was thirty-two. Still, every aspect, from symptoms to diagnosis to treatment, has been an exercise in corporeality and what it means for women. It took me a long time to be diagnosed, as it takes many people with endometriosis a long time, due to a combination of indifference from people who didn't menstruate and resigned stoicism from people who did. My friends told me incapacitating period pain was just something to be endured; my then-husband glazed over a little when I talked about it, the conversational equivalent of crossing your eyes to blur out something unpleasant. A few days out from surgery, I discovered he hadn't even looked up "endometriosis" on Wikipedia. He thought it might be upsetting.

Needing, having, and recovering from surgery will confront even the staunchest body-ignorer. I had to do a full colonoscopy-style prep beforehand, in case there was endometrium on my stomach or bowels; nothing challenges a person, or a partnership, that desperately wants to ignore the burden of bodies like having to shut yourself in the bathroom all night while you shit water. The pain after I got home was a crash course in the weird realities of anatomy. Much worse than the incision sites was the knifelike pain in my shoulder, caused by carbon dioxide bubbles fetching up under my diaphragm, pressing on a nerve. (This is normal after laparoscopic procedures but also *bonkers* to experience or even think about.) My recovery took longer than they told me it would. I found out only much later the surgery had been trickier than expected, because the rogue endometrium had gotten mixed up with some of the delicate pipeways around my bladder. As if someone talking about scraping uterine lining off your ureters wasn't stark enough, I was also issued a report that described every bit of removed matter—its color, size, consistency, and character. Part of me wishes I'd kept it, for the gory fascination. Instead, I barely read it and got rid of it right away. Who knew there were so many kinds of tissue in the uterus? Who wanted to?

I say I have "at least" one chronic illness because there's another one, polycystic kidney disease, which runs in my family. I have a one in two chance, a coin toss, but I have long avoided finding out whether it came up heads or tails. Mostly, when I'm not thinking about how I'm going to die of kidney failure in our dystopian future where health care no longer exists, I don't have a lot of emotional engagement with this possibility. At any rate, if you're going to die in a dystopian future, kidney failure is a nice quiet way to go. And yet. In one of my visits to those gruesome museums I love, I came upon a polycystic kidney—a preserved one, not wax. It was grotesquely inflated, bubbling with cysts, easily three or four times the size of the normal kidney on display. I go to medical museums a lot. I have seen fetuses too malformed to be viable, a distended human colon like an eight-foot cigar, a pair of pants made of skin. I've seen at least a hundred wax models of various things being eaten away by syphilis. I've flinched many times at these museums, but seeing that kidney, imagining it existing inside my own personal grudgingly tolerated body, is the only time I've cried in one.

This is why Scylla's story is so viscerally horrifying to me: The idea of looking down at a monstrous body and trying to get away, and then realizing that the monstrous body is yours. Is you.

∾

I usually like to kick against the demands of the patriarchy—it's kind of my thing—but in this case, we're on the same side. It is appalled by my body, and so am I. We both wish the whole thing would disappear. But the stories men have always told about women's bodies—the vagina dentata, the Venus with her gaping wound, the crotch exploding into dogs—are not meant for me, because these stories are never meant for me. I am the subject, not the audience. They are intended as a nudge to other men, a warning about women's disappointing carnality. When I wonder what Scylla's transformation must have been like for her, I am reading between the lines. This is what I'm supposed to get from that story: "But to the girdle do the gods inherit; Beneath is all the fiend's."

Nobody *really* likes to think about how we all ride around in vehicles of meat that are rotting underneath us for most of our lives, but for a straight man looking at a woman—or anyway, for the Male Gaze looking at a woman—that fact feels like not just a downer but a betrayal. Where are the poreless, depilated angels they were promised? The human body is a disappointment to us all, but for men it is rarely presented as more than it is: an unruly sack of fluids and stench. The images of women, at least women found desirable, have long been divorced from these realities. In rare instances, women who are both Cool and Hot are allowed to eat and burp, but that's really the limit. The most stark, embarrassing truths of the body, blood and pus and gas and fungus and smelling like fish and shitting yourself during childbirth, are at best a joke and at worst a kind of treachery. (This is why I have to appreciate scenes like the one in the 2011 film *Bridesmaids*, in which five women of varying degrees of conventional beauty have simultaneous violent diarrhea in a bridal store. I do not like this scene! I hate this scene. But I don't hate it even a fraction as much as the Male Gaze hates watching thin, blonde Kristen Wiig poop, and I take pleasure and solace in that.) Scylla's transformation is both joke and betrayal, in a way, as well as a punishment: an absurd and awful revelation that her body is more frightening than Glaucus was prepared to handle. It works, by the way. He falls out of love.

But who cares what Glaucus thinks? The one I care about in this story is the frightened girl standing on dogs gone mad: the one who suddenly knows, as I do, that her body is an abomination. I want to imagine her past as her future, to catch her in her futile flight from herself and turn her around to look at Homer's vision: the man-eater in her clifftop cave, beyond the reach of arrows. *Look*, I want to say, *even your rival Circe knows you're invincible now. No man can touch you.* Odysseus himself is not felled by Scylla, but neither does he defeat her; he wants to, but Circe scolds him, reminding him that he is only a man and Scylla is an immortal creature. The Scylla of Homer is so much more horrible than Ovid's—her rows of teeth, her impossible necks, her twelve feet dangling down. Horrible, and untouchable, and unbowed.

❧

My particular approach to the horrors of female embodiment—my personal fear of it, but more to the point, my culture's—is to try to disavow the whole thing. Other people cope with the same messaging by trying hard to mold their body to fit ideals—an impossible task, since the ideal is for their body to disappear entirely and be replaced with an airbrushed photo that can still do sex. Or they cope by trying to shift to a new rubric, optimizing their bodies for sports or weightlifting or having the most tattoos. Or maybe they cope by flaunting their imperfect forms, and simultaneously flaunting their willingness to be human and mammalian and immune to pressure. These are the ones I'm in awe of: the fat burlesque artists, the stretch-marked lingerie models, the regular-ass women in their bathing suits on Instagram like it isn't even a thing. Here are my monstrous groin-dogs, sorry not sorry if they eat you.

How do you do that? How do you mount to your cliffside cave, to lounge disgustingly and occasionally eat up any six men you choose? How do you trail your gross toes in the water and smile with your three rows of teeth, a hideous smile, because no one can touch you, because your horrible body is a triumph? How do you even imagine these things when you're still the girl standing in the water, frightened of dogs?

I suppose it starts when you stop running. I suppose it starts by looking down.

༄

I went to the Josephinum for the same reason I go to any museum of medicine: because I am fascinated by the absolute repulsiveness of the human corpus, and the way it is so often elevated to the realms of history and art. These museums both celebrate and thumb their noses at mortality. Most of us rot, but the Soap Woman at the Mutter Museum is still hanging around in Philadelphia, making people a little uncomfortable. The anatomical Venus, who was never alive but who represents the shocking grossness held in every beautiful form, spills her guts inside her glass box in perpetuity. The body is dead. Long live the body.

I think part of me believes that if I surround myself with these disgusting monuments, all the horrors of the body externalized, I will become— What? At peace with myself, I guess. But the women here don't fart or pee, and they smell like nothing but wax. They are not dying; they haven't even deteriorated over the two centuries since their birth. As gruesome as it is sometimes, a medical museum is a temple to the body's wonders, not its horrors. What's terrible about a disease is the way it progresses, not the skin lesions preserved in a wax moulage. What's terrible about a body is the way it traps you, the way it lets you down, the disgust and betrayal and vulnerability and inevitable, unstoppable decay. Whatever I want to find here isn't lying serene in the cases. It's walking among them, hideous and miserable and resigned.

SINGING FOR BREAD

THE FIRST THING YOU SEE is Alicia Silverstone picking a wedgie.

The video for Aerosmith's "Crazy" starts off with a shot of Catholic schoolgirl legs, an image that Britney Spears would make lascivious four years later in the video for " . . . Baby One More Time." Here, though, there's nothing sexual about them—no heels, no hiked-up skirt, just skinny calves and saddle shoes and a hemline that dips below fingertip length. Still faceless, she unselfconsciously adjusts her underwear (without displacing her sensible skirt), then ducks into the girls' bathroom. When the legs appear again, there's quite a lot more of them—Alicia's skirt is caught on the bathroom window she's shimmying out of—but even the glimpse below the skirt is almost chaste: improbably, she's wearing lace-edged tap pants, longer than most teens' shorts. (No wonder they were riding up.) She's also wearing a lace-edged tank top, as we find out a minute later when she hops into a car with her friend Liv Tyler, the Aerosmith singer's real-life daughter, and they both whip off their uniform shirts and toss them out of the car. The tanks are skimpier than their Oxford shirts, but utterly unsexualized; this scene is about pure freedom.

This purity is not because Alicia Silverstone and Liv Tyler aren't hot. Alicia Silverstone and Liv Tyler are, or at least were to me at age fourteen when this video came out, probably the hottest women alive. The innocence of those early scenes comes from the fact that their hotness in this video is never casually deployed. It's a firehose they turn on unsuspecting men to bowl them over, or arc over each other for the fun of it, like kids playing in hydrant spray. When they climb out of the window or throw their shirts from a moving car, they haven't turned it on yet. There just isn't anything, yet, that they need it for.

Suddenly it's dark, and the girls pull into a gas station. Alicia has changed into a very '90s slip dress, and Liv is wearing unforgettable leather pants. The raunchy old man outside leers at them, and Liv laughs; his lust is not a threat but an opportunity. The gentle stoner indoors simply gestures for them to take whatever they want: sunglasses, snacks. Liv Tyler puts an entire loaf of sliced bread in her purse. They peel out without paying for the gas—although not before handing the boy at the register a strip of topless pics from the photo booth as a show of gratitude. (You know, the standard gas station photo booth.)

This is the turning point: with men in the picture, and goods to be had, their sexuality becomes a tool. The next stop on the "Crazy" road trip is amateur night at a strip club that's offering a $500 first prize. Liv puts on an outfit reminiscent of her father's stagewear, kicks and writhes in a way that echoes his performance style. Or maybe the joke is that his style echoes hers, a forty-six-year-old man shaking his booty like a teen girl on the pole. The video gives young women ownership of many kinds of power, this one among them: the power to hold an audience.

Alicia Silverstone, unconvincingly dragged out in a suit and tie, looks on with a mixture of pride and lasciviousness. She's a stand-in for the male gaze, almost a parody, but as she shakes her hair free of her fedora, it's clear that she's also a focal point of seductive power: a black hole, collapsing temptation together with answering lust. Liv looks at no one else, plays to no one else, as if the male audience doesn't exist. She doesn't even take off her pants. And yet they win the contest, and get the prize. Just being in their event horizon, the indirect radiation of their beauty, makes the men hand over the cash. This kind of power, too, is granted them everywhere they go: to be given things, without question. It's akin to the power of stage charisma, and the power that turns admiration into desire.

The video ends with them flagging down a hot farmer, taking him skinny dipping, and driving away with his clothes. That's it. They just kidnap a hunk, get him naked, and make him chase down their car. When he finally catches up and jumps, fully nude, into the (already occupied) passenger seat, it's the only instance of physical contact between a man and woman in the video, and only because they're the ones who sought him out. On the final zoom out, his abandoned tractor is tracing the word "Crazy" in the corn. Men will abandon all sorts of responsibilities, all sense of dignity, for the chance at that moment of touch.

For a video featuring a flawless teen pole dancing, "Crazy" isn't really about the desires of straight men. Or rather, it's about them, but it's not *for* them; it's about how men's desire is a vulnerability, a handle pretty girls can wrench to open any door. It's part of a story we tell about a certain kind of power: the power of seduction, not sex but the unspoken promise of sex, for which you must pay in advance. It's part of a story about advertising, about who is a marketer and who is a mark, about how to package what you're offering and how to tell when someone bites. It's part of a story that starts in a walled garden at the beginning of the world, and winds through an ancient island near Italy where the Sirens sing their lonely song.

It's part of a story that confused me for the rest of my life.

My primary reaction to the video, which I saw exclusively in the middle of the night secretly bingeing MTV at someone else's house that had cable, was a sort of woozy, inchoate longing: a sense of powerfully wishing for something and knowing it was impossible, and also not being entirely sure what it was. I would never look like them. I would never have people who looked like them pay attention to me. I couldn't command that kind of power, and I couldn't be at its mercy. So which one was I mourning? Did I want to be the goddess or the offering?

❧

The dangerous seductress may be the most cross-culturally universal female monster there is. In Central America, she goes by different names in different countries—Sihuanaba, Cegua, Ciguapa—and appears as a long-haired bathing woman later revealed to have the face of a horse or a skull. South America has the Patasola in Colombia, a one-legged lurer and eater of men, and the singing Iara in Brazil. Some Native American tribes had stories of the Deer Woman, who might be a neutral or friendly spirit or might punish men tempted by her beauty away from their community and values. In Scandinavia, she may go by the name Huldra and have a shocking cow or fox tail and a back like a rotten tree. The beautiful Scottish glaistig may lure you with her song and drink your blood. And of course there's the succubus, a medieval Christian creation with roots in the Old Testament. She's a demon who seduces human men and, according to some chroniclers, steals their semen. Across the world, across the centuries, these fearsome creatures draw men into lust, and whatever consequences arise from lust: death, ostracism, or simply being made to look like a fool.

Though the method of temptation varies—a beautiful voice, a beautiful face, a beautiful body—the story is usually the same: the woman who seems so appealing is both dangerous and hideous. It's not clear which betrayal is worse: the eventual doom (devouring, exsanguination, gradual wasting away) or the discovery of the horse face, cow tail, bark back, missing leg. Seduction is seen as women's only weapon, our purpose, the thing that makes us real. But it also makes us a lie. It's a method of drawing men in with the promise of wish fulfillment, so by the time he notices your flaws, it's too late.

In ancient Greece, many monsters had beautiful women's faces. The monster often existed as a cautionary tale about what lurks behind the feminine facade. But monstrous seduction, specifically, came in the form of the Sirens, creatures with women's heads and the bodies of birds, whose singing entices sailors to leap into the sea and drown. There are generally three of them, sometimes two, and though their names vary, the translations are usually some variation of "Sings Great" or "Messes with Your Mind." That's their thing: sings great, messes with your mind.

There are three ways to escape the Sirens: plug your ears, hold yourself in place, or sing back louder. In *The Odyssey*, Odysseus's men take the first approach. On the advice of the enchantress Circe, they stuff their ears with wax at the first sign of the Sirens' song. Odysseus himself uses the second tactic, ordering his crew to tie him to the mast and tighten the bonds if he begs to be released. The Argonauts, who pass the same way on their voyage to find the Golden Fleece, have their own secret weapon: the musician

Orpheus, who chooses the third option, confounding the Sirens with a song of his own. (Still, one man jumps over the side.) If there are any other options for dealing with the Sirens, any way of rendering yourself immune to their power, we never hear about them. The power of their enticement is so strong that mental fortitude is not enough. You can keep yourself from hearing or keep yourself from moving, but that's all.

The Sirens were not beautiful, or anyway, it didn't matter if they were beautiful. (They're bird-women, but maybe you're into that.) The sailors who drowned for them never saw their faces. What the Sirens offered was something separate from beauty, though beauty is often one of its harbingers. They trafficked in temptation.

Temptation is not exactly beauty, and it's not exactly sex. It's the *promise* of sex, or the promise of something; we don't know the lyrics of the Sirens' song. Margaret Atwood, in her poem about the Sirens, imagines them offering the reassurance everybody longs for: "you are unique / at last." Mary Ruefle's poem "Deconstruction" has them singing the whole text of *The Odyssey*—what else but the story of his life could Odysseus find so compelling and so dangerous? This Mortal Coil's "Song to the Siren" (well, really Tim Buckley's, but I like the cover version) conjures up a hybrid promise of sex and painless death: "Sail to me, let me enfold you." Homer, who maybe has a little more authority in this matter, has them tempt Odysseus by promising to praise him and tell him the future—but Apollonius, who wrote of the Argonauts' voyage, doesn't tell us what they said at all. In William Morris's 1867 poem "The Death of Jason," also about the Argo, they sing about a world free of strife or aging or disease. And in *The Source of Magic*, a 1979 comic fantasy novel by the always at least slightly misogynistic Piers Anthony, the song of the Siren is "a distillation of the sex appeal of all womankind." These are all different facets of the same tempting jewel. What matters is the promise, the offer: here is something you want. It doesn't have to be sex, but it boils down to sex, the way anything fervently desired is sex at its core.

Perhaps more than any other story of female monstrousness, how you read the story of the Sirens depends on whose side you take. They are monsters, in the usual Greek antiquity sense, for their hybrid bodies, but are they made monstrous by the men's corpses that Homer says litter their little island? They didn't kill a single one. Those men jumped in of their own accord.

If a woman stands there singing, and her song is alluring, is it her fault if someone is inspired to launch himself over the side of a boat? How you answer that question depends in large part on where your sympathies lie. The chroniclers who spoke of the Sirens were fundamentally on the side of the questing heroes; it wouldn't have occurred to them to be otherwise. Weren't these men—Jason, Odysseus, Orpheus—the center of the story? From that angle, the Sirens are villains, waylaying adventurers and leaving them broken on the beach. But what about the view from the Sirens' island, watching the boats go by? What if we put them at the center? Then maybe the story is one of a flock of bird-women singing together, punctuated occasionally by a distant splash.

Or maybe it's the story of women for whom the ability to get a man's attention is a matter of life and death. Because here's the thing: The Sirens aren't doing this for fun. In some versions, an indifferent audience—someone who's able to hear them and pass unharmed—is doom to them. Odysseus triumphs over temptation: He hears their song and, bound to the mast, sails on. *The Odyssey* never concerns itself with the Sirens again. So what happens to the bird-women, left behind on their rock? According to some chroniclers, they either die immediately or throw themselves into the sea.

The popular conception of the Sirens gilds their seduction with a kind of vindictive delight: classical catfishes, getting a kick out of attracting the unwary. But what if it's actually an act of desperation? What if a Siren loses everything when her song fails?

❧

Culturally, we have a complicated relationship with seduction. In a sense, it's the primary form of power allowable to women, because it's a power predicated on men's desires. In another sense, it's seen as an amoral manipulation, an *abuse* of women's power. We knowingly exploit men's weaknesses, presenting ourselves as potential sexual conquests in order to bleed men dry. Having taken our fill, we turn out to fall short in some way.

Despite our performance, we're actually a less valuable prize than adver-
tised, or we're prudish, or a slut. (Somehow, there's nothing more disappointing to a man who decries women's sexual manipulation than actually
being willing to sleep with him.) The Huldra eventually turns around,
revealing the hollow tree.

The image of seductiveness as a kind of deception is all over the Western canon, from Shakespeare to Reddit. "I have heard of your paintings
well enough," snaps Hamlet. "God has given you one face and you make
yourselves another." Across the centuries, a man hunched in front of his
computer nods in sympathy: "That's why I take them swimming on the
first date." Makeup is a lie, a kind of chemical glamour spell that makes
women look more valuable than they are. Purity is a lie, an enticing challenge (many of the supposed literary masterpieces of the nineteenth century center around a man trying to talk, trap, or force a chaste young girl
into sleeping with him) that either becomes an obstacle—not a fun game
after all!—or evaporates, along with the value it imparts, once the game is
won. Overt sexuality is also a lie, a promise of easy pleasure that inevitably
turns out to be bait.

Like the culpability of the Sirens, the moral valence of seduction depends on your perspective. Are Liv and Alicia allowed a loaf of bread
because they are so pleasing to the eye, or are they extorting baked goods
from men who lie stunned and helpless before the misleading possibility
of sex? Or, the most complex and probably truest explanation: Are they
taking what they can get, because the expectation will be there anyway
and meanwhile the tribute keeps them fed? (It's no coincidence that some
commentators of late antiquity suggested that the Sirens were a metaphor
for sex workers, who also face censure for profiting from a demand they
did not create.) Temptation is a promise, but it's not always clear where
it's coming from: women making promises, or men using women to make
promises to themselves. And if you're feeding yourself with those free
loaves of bread you get for being seductive, then being seductive becomes
the way you survive.

When I mentioned the "Crazy" video to a friend recently, he said, "Oh wow, that's one of the founding texts of my sexuality." That's true of me too—but not just because of Liv and Alicia's glossy lips and perfect navels, appearing when I was just old enough to appreciate them and before it was (like now) creepy to appreciate them too much. Rather, stories about seduction were textbooks for me because they set up the winning conditions for being a girl. This is what it looks like to succeed in performing your gender: having men give you money for the best striptease, or stand by while you shove snacks in your purse, or let you drive off without paying for gas.

This idea—that it's possible for a woman to be so attractive that her beauty becomes an uncomplicated asset, never a danger to herself—is more or less pure fantasy. But it's a fantasy that underlies so many of the stories we tell about seduction as feminine power: the gold digger, the honeypot, the girl on the casting couch, all the women who use enticement to get their way. It's a foolish story, like all fantasies, delicately unhooked from a reality in which women's bodies are used, traded, and commodified without consent. But foolish stories have impact at that age, when you're old enough to have big feelings but too young to be sure how to interpret them. That vertiginous sensation when I watched Liv and Alicia, which might have been lust, might also have been revelation. Maybe this was what it felt like to learn how the world works.

Except for a magnetic moment on the strip club stage, the interactions *between* Alicia and Liv are fairly chaste. Though they clearly share a bed on their road trip, they're only shown in it pillow-fighting. If that was supposed to be a euphemism, I did not get it. To me, this was not a story about girls in a sexual relationship, or girls with whom a sexual relationship was even possible; it was a story about the way sex, or the promise of sex, could be somehow advantageous, even protective. I was wholly seduced by them, in the sense of being enchanted, but if you'd asked me, I probably wouldn't have said I wanted to have sex with them, or really do anything except watch from afar and maybe wave them off indulgently when they stole a loaf of bread. After all, such a scenario had no place in the game that was being set up for me. Without that framework—female seduction, male desire—how did you know if you'd won?

When the video came out, I was fourteen and a virgin. Not too long afterward, based largely on the intensity of my reaction to girls like Liv and Alicia (not always celebrities, but always a little distant and untouchable due to impossible coolness and beauty: a girl named Sarah from some after-school theater program, who was a head taller than me and whose breasts I am embarrassingly better able to conjure than her face; a girl named Elly from my high school who was much too cool for me to talk to and who I once spotted in a local vintage shop in a shirt that would absolutely not have passed our public school's dress code, an image that remains burned into my brain), I started openly identifying as bisexual. Not too long after that, I stopped.

It wasn't that my feelings had changed—in fact, it was kind of the opposite. Though I continued being intensely fascinated with specific women, and women's bodies generally, I also found these fascinations paralyzing. When I was interested in a boy, there was a drive to action: I generally wanted to sleep with them as quickly as possible, to prove I could. That was the game, after all. When I was interested in a girl, whatever that interest really meant, I froze. It was like a chess piece drifting off the board. What do we do out here? What are the rules?

I let crushes on men take over my life, because I understood the goal: Prove your worth through seduction. (I rarely did.) Crushes on women brought mostly confusion and fear, but at least they didn't demand anything of me. I had nothing to prove, as long as I made no claims. I never started thinking of myself as "straight," but calling myself queer seemed at best misleading, at worst stolen valor.

I am, in general, a little allergic to declarations of identity. I tend to describe myself in terms of things I *do* and am uncomfortable making claims about what I *am*. But this reticence is particularly vexed, and particularly stark, when it comes to sex and gender. Of *course* I'm attracted to women. Have you *seen* women? I'm just not really sure what, if anything, that attraction *means*. If my identity is based on what I do, then I have to grapple with the fact that I haven't, pardon the expression, *done* women. More-over, the reasons for that—my own issues—still apply. I have anxiety and body shame about the idea of sleeping with women in a way I've never had with men, partly because I don't care as much what men think, but largely because attractive men don't represent, in their very attractiveness, all the ways in which I've failed. In fact, the more attractive I find a woman, the less attractive I feel in her presence: oversized, awkward, lumbering, gross. (I also assume, with absolutely no evidence, that she'll project *her* inse-curities on *me*—that I'll represent the ways she also could have failed but didn't.) If Alicia the Siren is the winning condition of femininity—given bread and money for the mere potential represented by her body, then plucking the hunk who pleases her from among the corn—then where does someone like me belong in that story? At best offscreen.

Maybe most importantly, the idea of being attracted to women feels somehow tainted, a compromised scientific sample. How can I tell what I feel about women when every single aspect of my culture, from advertis-ing to ancient Greek myth, is telling me I want to fuck them?

There is, I suppose, an argument to be made that I should just get over myself and identify as queer, for the sake of visibility. But what does that visibility achieve? Other people's perfectly reasonable answers—generally, that it's their identity and it matters that other people know that—never feel like they apply to me. That's great if you have a strong sense of who you *are*, but what does it say about what you *do?* Calling myself queer doesn't signal availability; I am married and, furthermore, deeply neu-rotic. It doesn't change my commitment to the idea that queer people of all stripes deserve all relevant human rights and, beyond that, all rele-vant courtesy and kindness. I would hope that's obvious, and besides, you shouldn't need to be a member of a group to care about it. All it does is tell people I like to look at boobs. But that's the thing: We pretty much all like to look at boobs. They're *boobs*. Women's bodies are so desperately over-freighted as objects of seduction and desire that you can't possibly come to them clean.

I obviously have a strong reaction to feminine-coded bodies, and seek them out. You need only look at my Instagram activity to see that. (Please don't.) But that reaction could be envy, or platonic admiration, or a masochistic desire to beat myself over the head with my failure to achieve the expected level of seductiveness. Or it could be a different kind of desire: the desire to vicariously live the "Crazy" life, being showered with sunglasses and Twizzlers and prizes and praise. In the founding texts of my sexuality, the aim of seduction is not just attention but care. Being a trophy means being taken care of. If no one wants you, you're on your own.

What does it mean to respond to the Siren's song? If I jump in and drown, is it because I wanted whatever the song promised? Or is it because I wanted to reach that untouchable rock, to stand there and tempt men to their doom?

There is genuine power in seductiveness, and though there's danger too, the danger sometimes feels like it belongs in another story. There's a reason that sexual enticement is both expected and demonized. If it held no power, we wouldn't have so many stories about why seductive women should be feared. Unlike many of the other qualities they use to make monsters of us—ugliness, anger, voraciousness—seduction is also genuinely rewarded. You can make money off it, if you're willing to assume the risks of that work. You can use it to get your way.

I was not sure in 1994, and I'm still not sure, whether I wanted Liv and Alicia or simply wanted the permissions and power that the world, at least in the confines of the video, granted them. This is common to the point of cliché—"Do I want to fuck her, or do I want to be her?"—and it is, I think, common for a reason. If any fervent desire is a kind of horniness, then it makes sense for lust and envy to be nearly indistinguishable. Both are an urge to get inside someone's skin. And both will addle you, daze you, make you jump into the ocean and drown. The Sirens offer hope for every kind of horniness, draw out every kind of desire. But there's no guarantee you'll survive what they're offering you.

There is genuine power in seductiveness. It's not a power I have, but it's a power I'm susceptible to. Of all the monsters of myth, the Siren is the one I feel the least kinship with. I am more likely to be her victim. But maybe that's only because there's no other space for me in the story: a story of hero versus monster, of temptation versus resolve. Maybe if the Sirens were singing to each other, for each other, everything would change.

There are more serious consequences to our culture's love-hate obsession with female seduction than one person feeling awkward all through Pride Month because she wants to buy a bralette with rainbow back straps and doesn't know if it's okay. (I didn't, and it's sold out now, and I know Pride is overcommercialized, leave me alone.) Notably there's the way that feminine seductiveness, engineered by and for men, gets turned retroactively into an excuse when those same men overstep. (*How was he supposed to help himself, when the temptation was so great?*) This is one of the great injustices perpetrated against women: we are blamed for our abuse, based on the same behaviors and self-presentation we are trained to use to keep ourselves pleasing and favored. (*Why did you dress that way, why did you smile, why didn't you slap and scream?* Because I was told being sweet and pretty would keep me safe.)

But it's also sobering, to me, that we so often don't know what our faces look like, what our songs sound like, free of that gaze. That if we're not a man in a boat, or a man in the water, or the woman standing with corpses at her feet, we don't know where we belong. The Sirens are the only women in that story.

Here's another embarrassing revelation: When women talk about being harassed or catcalled or groped, I often feel wistful, even envious. This is a fucking stupid thing to think, and I'm not by any means proud of it, though I think I'm also not alone. I know, intellectually, that these instances of male attention are violating or, at a minimum, unpleasant. I don't actually want to deal with them, ever, and I've hated the few occasions when I did. It's a poisonous, or more accurately, a poisoned mindset. We live in a culture where women's worth is predicated on the pleasure they bring to men, and that has a way of seeping into your groundwater. In such a culture, these intrusions come as proof that you are an appealing temptation, and that you therefore deserve to exist. This is how you earn your personhood: by gaining men's sexual approval, which is no less valuable when it's expressed as an onslaught. At very least, you are supposed to avoid the chilly but peaceful hell of men's sexual indifference.

Seduction, in this framework, is a route to full humanity. If you want to be seen as a person, you must lure them in with sex, revealing your needs and feelings only once the trap is set. Even then, humanity in a sexual prize is ironically monstrous—that's the fox tail, the horse face, the draining of life energy or the leap into the sea. The seductress reveals herself as a monster—which is to say, not just an image, not just a fantasy. But without the hook of seductiveness, you are out in the cold: no blood, no bread.

The Sirens were once handmaidens to Persephone, an agricultural goddess. After she was kidnapped by Hades, ruler of the underworld, they were given wings—either as an asset or a punishment, depending on which story you choose. Per Ovid, they asked for flight in order to help Persephone's mother search for her. Per Pseudo-Hyginus, they were transformed into bird-women as revenge for their inattention.

But I wonder if the story might have gone the other way, if it hadn't been told by men. What is the Siren's version of the Sirens' tale? Once upon a time, there were three sweet birds singing together, singing for themselves, on a rock alone—until human men passing by thought their song was desirable, and blessed or cursed them for it with a human face. From then on, they were people, but only a little bit: only as far as the delight men could extract from them. From then on, they sang to survive.

※

It's difficult, maybe even impossible for us to imagine an understanding of women's seductiveness untouched by the male gaze—which is to say, not only the appraising looks of actual men, but the patriarchal panopticon that judges women's bodies according to some baroque standard of feminine appeal. When people say they get dressed up or do their makeup solely for their own benefit, because they "like to look good," there is always a murmur at the back of my mind saying "good according to who?" (Actually, it says "according to whom," but I want you to think I'm cool.) Does lipstick "look good" in an objective sense? Does makeup, in general, "look good"? This uncertainty persists despite the fact that I put much more effort into my look when hanging out with women than with men, despite the fact that my own going-out looks often include elements (grey lipstick, black eyelids) that aren't generally considered feminine or pretty. The *immediate* audience may not be men, but who set the cultural preference for everything I try to mimic when dressing up: curves, big eyes, full lips, youth? And by the same token, if I find a woman's face or body beautiful, or if I assume she won't think the same of me, is that an uncomplicated mirror of my heart? Or is it the patriarchy speaking through me, telling me who has value and who succeeds?

What faces do the Sirens see when they look at each other, instead of being looked at by human men? What songs, what lyrics do they hear? We may never know, because the assumed audience of men is a matter of life and death to creatures who are doomed to die when ignored. But those men never see them in the stories—they hear and die, or they don't hear and live, or they're Odysseus, but they never lay eyes on the singers. The Siren in the myth is just a song.

Maybe that's the whole point—that she's a song and not a body. Where, in this story, would a real person live? The role of seductress, which seems so desirable, even mandatory for women, leaves no place for a woman to actually inhabit it. Like so many other required roles, all the knife-thin ridges we walk between monster and nonentity, it is an unlivable space, an airless plane into which we try to project our unruly three-dimensional selves. That's the secret story of the monstrous temptress: her image is tantalizing, but her body is a horror. The Siren takes this even further. She is a beautiful song annealed to a monstrous form, but even her body is a whisper of hearsay, never seen by man. And the other Sirens? They see her, but we have no language for what they see.

This is the Siren's true, untapped power—not her allure, but her invisibility. Spun from men's fantasies, measured by her ability to tempt them, she still resists being fully pinned down by the story. The myth tells men what to fear, but never shows them. The monster is hidden, her song ever-changing, fitting itself to whatever promises men make to themselves about women, whatever words they want to hear. We are told how to listen to the Siren, or how to avoid listening, but not how to look at her. The landscape of that shrouded island, the details of faces and wings, are still there to be written: a protected space unshaped by the patriarchal gaze.

Maybe monsters get to learn how to look at each other, how to see what the stories tell us not to see. Maybe anyone could be there, in the mists, on the rocks, singing for nobody, singing for herself.

THE SNATCHERS

THE HARPIES WERE ESPECIALLY FOUL, even as grotesqueries go. Virgil writes in *The Aeneid*, "No monster is more malevolent than these, no scourge of gods or pestilence more savage ever rose from the Stygian waves." The creatures are mostly bird, with the faces of women. Like many creatures of myth, their monstrousness comes in part from being two things at once, and like many female monsters it comes specifically from the fact that they are both a woman and *something else*, something that horrifies simply because its girl-face is a misleading trap. A whole lot of monsters, both in Greek antiquity and in other traditions, can be summed up as "What a pretty lady! Now time to take a big sip of my coffee and look at the rest of her body."

But the horror of the Harpies goes beyond their hybridity. "These birds may wear the face of virgins, but their bellies drip with disgusting discharge, and their hands are talons, and their features pale and famished," writes Virgil. That's the Allen Mandelbaum translation. John Dryden's translation says they have "virgin faces, but with wombs obscene," which probably says more about Dryden than anything else. Beyond that physical grossness, though, the Harpies are defined by their thieving nature. It's right there in the name, from *harpezein*, or "snatcher." In Homer, they're not even bird-women yet, but they're already thieves—storm spirits who carry people off unawares. But the defining story of the harpies is the one canonized in the journey of the Argonauts, in which the vile creatures are sent to torment King Phineus of Thrace. Any time Phineus is served food, the creatures swoop down and claw it away, either devouring it or rendering it inedible with their disgusting smell. They are ravenous, but their appetite isn't just for food. What they can't eat, they are content to merely destroy. The important thing is that their target goes hungry.

Phineus and the quest for the Golden Fleece is not the last we hear of the Harpies. In *The Aeneid*, the Harpies are no longer tormenting Phineus, but hanging out on an island where Aeneas and his crew make landfall. Aeneas, narrating, fondly recalls discovering the cows and goats wandering "unguarded." The crew kills as many of the cattle as they want to eat and a few more to share with the gods. But then the Harpies swoop in, "plundering our banquet with the filthy touch of their talons." Aeneas and his men are incensed by this foul attack on their rightfully stolen property. Hopped up on vengeance, they chase down the Harpies, hacking fruitlessly at the creatures' blade-proof skin with their swords.

It does not occur to Aeneas and his men to wonder about the ownership of the meal they're fighting to defend. But in fact, the Harpy Celaeno says, the slaughtered cattle belonged to her and her sisters. The island where the crew was making merry, feasting on their stolen cows, was the kingdom of the Harpies' father. The sailors were the interlopers; the monsters were there by right. The Harpies weren't spoiling Aeneas's feast for fun—or, as in the case of Phineas, at the behest of the gods. They had come not to perpetrate a theft but to avenge it.

And yet it makes no difference, in the end, that the men were trespassers and thieves, that the Harpies belonged on the island and owned the cattle. As soon as the ship touched down, as soon as the men spied turf they could rest on and meat they could chase down, any woman's attempt to snatch it back became a monstrous overreach. A man who lays claim to unguarded property is a hero. A woman who grasps for her share is an abomination.

This is why calling a woman a harpy is more barbed than calling her a bitch. A Harpy is vicious and disgusting, yes, but she's more than that. She's someone who grabs for what doesn't belong to her (even if, as with the cows in *The Aeneid*, it does). To call a woman a harpy is both to deride her ambition and to reinforce the idea that she deserves nothing, that everything she's ever earned has been stolen from the mouths of men, to whom it truly belonged. It's a term especially weaponized against women who seek advancement in male-dominated fields like politics, and no surprise. If Hillary Clinton or Elizabeth Warren is a harpy—and both have been called a harpy many times, both sincerely in the right-wing media and acerbically in *Wonkette*—that's not only because she's vicious and shrill, but because she viciously and shrilly seeks to rise above her station. She aspires to a role that's not meant for her, a position she can only steal, not earn.

Though the Harpies descend on Phineus's food like wild animals, they are not wild animals. A vulture that scavenged or befouled food would not be monstrous; feral creatures eat where they can and shit where they must. There are two things that make a Harpy a monster, not a beast: her single-minded focus on depriving others, and her human female face.

❧

In late June 2019, the British tabloid the *Daily Mail* ran an article asking whether two players on the US Soccer team about to compete in the World Cup semifinals were, in the words of the headline, "just TOO arrogant." There were not many details provided about how this arrogance asserted itself, though the affront seemed to be mainly that the team had scoped out what hotel they might stay in if they advanced to the finals. Too arrogant for *what* wasn't specified, either; nobody was saying that the players' egos would affect their sports performance or lose them endorsement deals. The article did end with the implication that trust in their own prowess could make the team too lazy to win it all, but this is such a nakedly ridiculous thing to say if you've ever heard any athlete talk that the author couldn't bring himself to frame it as an actual claim, instead mealy-mouthing that "it is not inconceivable that complacency and hubris prove fateful." The point wasn't really that the players were too arrogant to win, anyway; it was just that they were too arrogant, generally. That there was an amount of arrogant it was acceptable for multimillionaire multi-champion sports stars to be, and they were *too*.

It should not come as a surprise, then, that the players under fire, Alex Morgan and Megan Rapinoe, were from the US *Women's* National

Team—which did not in fact get complacent, but instead went on to win the World Cup, again. (The lineup changes, of course, but the women's team has won four World Cups and four Olympic gold medals in the less than forty years since women were first allowed to compete in soccer at an international level. The men's team, for what it's worth, has won zero World Cups, though it did reach the semifinals once back in 1930. There are mitigating factors here—twice as many teams compete in the men's World Cup than the women's—but when you're calculating bragging rights, take those numbers into account.)

One should give the *Daily Mail* negative credit in areas like factual accuracy or moral compass; it is nakedly devoted to creating emotional responses at the expense of anything approaching reliable journalism, and is consistently anti-immigrant, anti-Muslim, anti-gay, dismissive towards women, and pro-fascist (as in, literally supported the Fascists in World War II). But for these same reasons, it can be an effective barometer of conservative beliefs—or at least what powerful conservatives think The Common Man *should* believe. All of the same can be said of another Rapinoe detractor, Donald Trump. (Well, he wasn't yet born during WWII, but all the rest.)

Trump took a dislike to Rapinoe after she said that she wouldn't go to "the fucking White House" if invited. In an error-laden but otherwise fairly mild (for him) string of tweets, Trump scolded, "Megan should WIN first before she TALKS!" Could have been worse—but as with the *Mail*, the message was clear. By imagining that they might win a competition (for which they were already in the quarterfinals! It's not like this was some big-dreaming kiddie league, or the men's team, or something!), these female athletes were overstepping their bounds. Proper behavior, apparently, was to soberly plug away with no expectation or even hope that one might ever succeed.

A few weeks later, Trump launched a much more characteristically awful series of Twitter barbs at a group of young female nonwhite members of Congress who had come to be known, rather distressingly, as "The Squad." Representatives Alexandria Ocasio-Cortez, Ilhan Omar, Ayanna Pressley, and Rashida Tlaib, he tweeted, should "go back and help fix the totally broken and crime infested places from which they came" before daring to criticize anything about the United States, the country they were democratically elected to govern. While "from which they came" seems suspiciously grammatically sophisticated for the president, the rest of the tweet thread was classic Trump: false claims (three of the women were born in the US) and blatant racism (only white people can be or deserve to be Americans). Tucked within the racism was a bonus nugget of misogyny: Women whose *job* it is to help run the country don't have the authority to point out its flaws. The representatives, Trump ranted, were "loudly and viciously telling the people of the United States, the greatest and most powerful Nation on earth, how our government is to be run." Minus the adjectives and hyperbole, this could be a description of the role of Congress. But for some mysterious reason—or two nonmysterious reasons—when these women wielded their duly elected power, the result was "vicious" and needed to be put down.

Alexandria Ocasio-Cortez, the de facto leader of The Squad (mostly because she's so skilled at popping off with well-sourced zingers on social media), had already allied herself with Megan Rapinoe. After the athlete expressed her disinclination to go to the fucking White House, AOC invited her on Twitter to tour the fucking House of Representatives. (She didn't say "fucking"! Actually, until AOC got there, I would have said the House of Representatives definitively does *not* fuck.) Rapinoe tweeted back, "Consider it done." It's not too surprising that two ambitious women, both stars in their respective fields, should respect each other—or join forces to irritate a powerful man. Harpies travel in flocks, after all. (Or teams, or squads.) But even without this public alliance, the two would have been linked by their treatment—by the president, by the president's supporters, and by the conservative media.

I have a bad habit of looking at the replies to public figures' tweets, in order to get a sense of what the most embarrassing people across the political spectrum are thinking, and what was striking to me during late June and early July 2019—call it the Month of the Harpy—was how much Trump fans' reactions to Rapinoe and AOC sounded the same. Both were criticized for having swelled heads, for craving attention, for getting above their station. (That quarter frequently derides AOC as "just a bartender," as if a humble Real Working American becoming a national leader weren't the plot of several beloved movies starring white men. Mr. Smith may go to Washington, but Ms. Ocasio-Cortez should remember her place.) Most of these critics would doubtless have protested against being called sexist, racist, or homophobic (Rapinoe is gay). They just happened to think that a couple of famous, skilled, influential women should be just a *little* less confident, a little more demure.

Does it even need to be mentioned that Trump is an incompetent brag-gart, a man who never understands the question but always answers by saying he's the best? Of course the standards are different for him. The standards have been different for him and his ilk all the way back to Ae-neas: the men who tell stories of themselves and each other as heroes. The men who own the cattle because they claimed the cattle, and fight off any foul monster who tries to take them back. The men who think defending what they've stolen means they owned it all along.

❧

Even the most motivated women don't usually want to be Harpies. A Harvard University study on business school students, published in March 2017, found female students downplay career aspirations and assertiveness in order to perform well on the "marriage market." (That's the term the researchers used.) The subjects, newly admitted graduate students in busi-ness, were asked to rate their ambition and leadership qualities, and to de-scribe desired compensation and willingness to work long hours and travel for a job. When they thought their answers were private, single and mar-ried women gave similar answers. When they thought their classmates—including men—would see the results, the single women students rated themselves lower on leadership and ambition, said they'd be willing to work fewer hours and travel less, and asked for a much lower yearly salary. Another related study showed that single women chose less career-driven hypothetical jobs after being told single men would see their results.

Why would ambition, leadership, desire for more pay hurt women in the "marriage market"? Because every minute a woman gives to her career is a minute she's taking away from her husband and her family duties. Because salaries, work travel, career-mindedness are the natural province of men. Because men own women's time, and men own success. They may parcel it out to us like an allowance, but grab the whole wad Jane Jetson–style and you're morally suspect at best. The wage gap is sometimes explained away by pointing out that women tend to choose less demanding jobs. It's not a sufficient explanation—women are also paid less than men for the same job—but insofar as it's true, this is why: because matching with men ambition for ambition is seen as greed and theft.

Making money, of course, is not the only valid kind of ambition. But it makes for a good case study, because in a society devoted to capitalism, career and financial goals are celebrated above all other aspirations. Consider everything that Americans are willing to toss away in the pursuit of money: leisure, family, ethics, compassion, rational behavior. And yet here is a point beyond which even the most financially ambitious women, who have put time and personal debt into the pursuit of career success, aren't willing to go. Paying $160,000 for your MBA education? Sure! Selling what integrity you have for a job with Monsanto or whatever? I guess! But having men *see* you seek status and money? That's foul. That's grasping for something you can only have through theft.

The same thing happens with the drive for political success—again, only one form of ambition, but one that is roundly celebrated in our culture as long as it comes from men. According to the Brookings Institution, though women in political power perform just as well as men, far fewer women run in the first place. The public policy organization's 2008 research suggested there were a few factors at work in this "ambition gap," among them the fact that women "are less likely than men to perceive a fair political environment." They're also less likely to think they're qualified—because we're not supposed to be arrogant—and less likely to be told they should run even if they're not. What Brookings didn't investigate was the public perception of female politicians by men. But a study two years later, by researchers from Yale and the University of Queensland, found that people—not just men—reacted to a female politician described as "power-seeking" with feelings of anger, disgust, and contempt. Power-seeking men were seen as assertive and competent. When women "perceive an unfair political environment" and decide not to run at all, this is what they perceive: the thinly veiled outrage that accompanies any woman's move towards political power, which is always seen as piracy.

Or forget money and power, and look at the prominence of women in literature. Though women read *and* write more than men, they have never come anywhere near parity in the academic canon, or the major book review sections, or the literary awards. An outside observer might be tempted to wonder whether women were simply less accomplished writers—until that outside observer realized that the academic departments and book review sections and literary awards committees have been for decades or centuries dominated by men. The choice to recognize or even publish women was for a long time made exclusively by men, and those men didn't appreciate glory-snatching harpies trying to steal their slots in the Intro to Literature syllabus, or the Man Booker longlist, or the "Most Anticipated Books of the Year."

Here's a case study. In 2015, a group of disgruntled (mostly) men calling themselves the Rabid Puppies decided to take a stand against the menace of "pink science fiction," which is to say, science fiction that is not written by white men, or that caters to or includes or even considers the perspectives of people who aren't white men. The Rabid Puppies, an angrier outcropping of the similarly disgruntled "Sad Puppies" who preceded them, were led by a man called Vox Day (real name: Theodore Beale), the kind of charmer who had described his crusade thus: "Pink SF is an invasion. Pink SF is a cancer. Pink SF is a parasitical perversion. Pink SF is the little death that kills every literary subgenre. And Pink SF isn't limited to SF; there is a very good reason the Sports Guy's meme 'Women Ruin Everything' applies so perfectly to most forms of literature. . . . Pink SF is the girls coming to play in the boys' sandbox and then shitting in it like cats." (Women writers, he noted, were acceptable as long as they stuck to "pillow books," the only appropriate genre for ladies.) This was the danger Day vowed to expunge: the Harpies swarming on men's rightful property and befouling what they could not steal.

Murasaki Shikibu invented the novel. Mary Shelley invented science fiction. But for Vox Day and his ilk, the presence and influence of women and minorities in the genre world was a monstrous imposition on territory they rightfully owned. The result was a massive coordinated attempt to game the democratic Hugo Awards nomination process by voting en masse to nominate a slate of white men, chosen by Day. (Awards committees made up of a small panel of celebrated writers have a tendency to perpetuate imbalances—if all your celebrated writers are white men, then your awards nominees will tend to be white men too, which means your celebrated writers are white men, ad infinitum. Vote-based awards nominations skirt this issue, but present other problems—for instance, they're exploitable.) When it came time to vote, the sci-fi community rejected this manipulation, but they mostly had to do it by voting "No Award" in every category dominated by Puppy appointees—meaning that the Rabid Puppies didn't win, but neither did anybody else. Vox Day and his followers were willing to taint the Hugo Awards, one of the primary engines of recognition in the genre they supposedly loved, rather than let women or minorities get their talons in. But sure, it's *girls* who shit in the sandbox.

My friend Meredith Yayanos tells similar stories about her experience in the New York music scene in the early 2000s. "It was just a given that us 'more serious' female musicians would need to work three times as hard as the men just to prove we were 'more than just a piece of ass,' as one dirtbag punk rock reed player who came to see a show of mine put it (thinking he was paying me a compliment)," she told me in an email. "So many of my feminine peers had similar experiences. So many of us got passed over for more prestigious gigs and mentorships in favor of dudes with half the skills." Mer is a highly trained musician and an expert in, among other things, the theremin, an electronic instrument that is trivial to play badly and very, very difficult to play well. (You know the Lev Grossman series *The Magicians*, in which the key to magic is the extremely precise execution of nearly impossible hand gestures? It's like that.) She was almost guaranteed to be better trained and a better natural musician than any of the men who challenged her. It didn't matter. "I can't tell you how many times a man would look up from his own instrument, upon hearing me play for the first time, and exclaim, in shock, 'Wow, you're really good!'" she told me. "Fuck yeah, I'm really good, ya dipshit! I've worked my whole life to get this far. Haven't you? But that's the thing. A lot of them hadn't. They just felt entitled to be there, taking up space and holding court."

The route these condescending men offered her into success—or whatever level of success they deigned to give her—was being charismatic, delicate, feminine, and available. "Twentysomething-year-old Mer let herself be convinced that the price of admission to this male-dominated world of professional music was to make sure I was attractive and poised enough," she told me. And of course, after she wore herself literally to the bone with an eating disorder, trying to earn back what was already rightfully hers, they still didn't want to let her into the secret room. "I fought for years to prove myself to these men more than to myself, which was, of course, futile and soul-crushing," she said. "I got spoken to like a child and treated like a performing monkey." She distanced herself from the music scene—and eventually rebirthed herself as a monster.

Recently, Mer has been making what she calls "doomsday disco" music under the name The Harpy. For her, the Harpy is "a state of being" or a "modality," incandescently furious but active and lucid, that was brought on by realizing how many men in her orbit—many of them artists and musicians—were habitually using, insulting, devaluing, and assaulting women. "Most of the ones who weren't outright breaking any laws were disturbingly comfortable indulging in all kinds of verbal harassment and abuse," she wrote to me. "Men would behave badly, would pride themselves on being addicts and assholes, and then we'd get blamed, gaslit, discarded. Called crazy or dirty. They might be rapists, but we were the ones befouled." The true offense, as always, is women laying claim to what men see as their due.

❧

Most people are not Vox Day; they don't explicitly say, or think, that women ruin everything. But our very ideas about what it means to be skilled or talented—in business and politics, but no less in the arts—is predicated on men performing maleness for men. In a similar way, but perhaps even more so, it is predicated on white people performing whiteness for white people. I once published an essay by author and editor Karissa Chen, in which she described being humiliated by her white writing workshop classmates for praising a story they found maudlin and overwrought. The author? Edwidge Danticat. When Chen found out later that Danticat was a beloved and decorated writer, she realized that the problem was not her taste but the way a white audience responded to something not written with them in mind—at least, when they hadn't been informed that it was widely considered a work of genius, even by the white literary establishment. (Danticat had won a MacArthur award, commonly called a "genius grant," shortly before, but Chen's classmates didn't know that, which meant she got to see their unvarnished reactions.) "What gets published, what's deemed worthy—these are things selected by gatekeepers whose standards of what passes for 'good' are rooted in their own worldview, histories, and traditions," she wrote. "When they deem something 'not good' instead of recognizing that they simply *don't understand it* because it hails from a different literary and cultural tradition, a cycle is perpetuated where the same 'acceptable' work gets made over and over again—and anything else is derided." Danticat managed to break through with talent and toughness and probably luck, but how many other writers either gave up or compromised?

A similar thing happens with gatekeepers who are men (as most of them are): their idea of what's "good" is defined by what they've seen before, what they understand, what's meant for them. There *are* some visual arts in which women routinely get their due, but those are generally downgraded to "crafts," for exactly that reason: if great art is the territory of men, then the territory of women must be something else. And make no mistake, great art is the territory of men. They have marked it. Man made God in his image, and for an encore, went on to create Art in his image too. That's the way of men, after all: Land on something and say it's yours, that it's for you. Who cares if the Harpies were already there? They no longer belong here. Chase them off when they come.

❧

It's tricky to argue in favor of ambition, because it's so often used to mean the desire for things—money, power, fame—that are also hooked in with the worst aspects of human civilization. At some point, praising ambition risks running into a version of that famous tweet: "Conservatives: Let's round up Muslims and put them in camps. Liberals: HIRE MORE WOMEN GUARDS." (The original tweet, by the no-longer-extant user @historyinflicks, has a clapping hands emoji between every word in "hire more women guards," a significant part of the humor but hard to reproduce in book form.) Women are underrepresented in finance and politics, true; they are also underrepresented among serial killers, but nobody's going to agitate about that one. But I think it's important to reclaim our ability to *aspire*, even if that means some people will aspire to dubious goals. Because punishing ambition, punishing the ability to aspire to *anything* without being made into a grasping monster, fundamentally restricts the imagination—the world you're able to picture, and the way you're able to picture your place in it. If we can't wish for power or success under the current structure, if we can't imagine even that amount of change, how can we possibly envision something better? Besides, inequality may be baked into our flawed system, but it isn't bounded there. Any new order designed by people who can't take a woman (or any disenfranchised person) seriously as a voice of power is only going to look like liberation for a few. That's oppression in a different hat, with a bigger beard.

And ambition is larger than the desire for material success or political clout, or even the desire for recognition in arts or sports or scholarship. To the patriarchy, even the wish to control our own bodies reads like ambition. As with business, and politics, and literature, our culture treats women's bodies as by rights the domain of men. This means that any progress we make towards reclaiming our most intimate property meets with the same kind of anti-Harpy horror, the fear of women trespassing on and befouling what is men's sole privilege to trespass on and befoul.

On a policy level, powerful men stand in judgment of our right to decide whether or not we will be pregnant, designating themselves as the rightful arbiters and characterizing those who object as sluts and murder-ers. Even before the Trump era, which has emboldened the GOP to openly fantasize about obliterating the rights of pregnant people to determine the use of their own wombs, there was a parade of legislative decisions made with zero input from women or people with uteruses, including Darrell Issa's all-male committee hearing on contraception coverage in 2012 and the all-male congressional panel that advanced a twenty-week abortion ban in 2013. In 2017, Mike Pence convened an all-male meeting to discuss a health bill that would strip reproductive and maternal coverage. Women and others who demand jurisdiction over our own uteruses, the ability to choose whether we are impregnated or impregnatable, are treated as interlopers. We are going against both nature and ethics, apparently, by influencing whether we use our bodies as incubators. The natural order of things is that the disposition of your uterus is controlled by a panel of men.

On an interpersonal level, men throw tantrums when they are not allowed to touch us as they please. The most high-profile examples are "incels," young men who identify as "involuntarily celibate" and blame women's sexual stinginess for everything from their unhappiness to vio-lence. At least half a dozen mass murders have been committed either by self-described incels or by men who pointed to lack of sexual attention as the reason for their crimes, and subsets of the incel community cele-brate mass murder and rape or fantasize about government-mandated fe-male sexual service. But the same pattern repeats in a million less-extreme ways: the man who gets angry or sulky when you're too tired or sick, the man who jokes about "converting" a lesbian, the man who keeps pressing until you give in. And men are always giving each other permission and approval for asserting their authority over the bodies we think are ours, based on his bright future or his glorious career or our short skirts.

Men legislate our bodies according to their personal preference and beliefs, and vilify us when we demand a say. Men grant themselves and each other the right to touch us, and attack us for denying them that sov-ereignty. Men shrug when we are physically threatened or hurt, then trot our bodies out as political human shields when it suits them: *We can't have trans women in women's bathrooms. What about my daughter?* For women to have full autonomy is for men to be deprived of their sex objects, their incubators, their trump cards. We are the Harpies swooping down to steal the spoils, and we are the cows.

❧

The guys going to meetings with Mike Pence, or using our physical safety as a political pawn, probably find no shame in saying that women are inferior. Hell, Mike Pence won't even eat lunch with a woman unless she brings a chaperone. But the fear of Harpies infects even those who think of themselves as the good guys, the staunch promoters of justice. So many people believe in gender equality, as long as reaching equality doesn't mean taking anything from men. As long as women stay within their rightful territory, defined as "all the territory men didn't annex for themselves."

We could all get along if women would take only what men wanted to cede them. We would all be okay with women writing their little books if they didn't try to win awards. We would all vote for a woman, just not *that* woman. We all believe the victim, until she accuses someone we know, or follow on Twitter, or watch on TV. The problem, we are told, is not that a woman asks for something—power, body autonomy, money, recognition, self-determination. It's that she snatches it out of the hands of men. Equality must be granted to those who have less, but not at the expense of those who have more. The Harpy wants to win, which means a man must lose. She wants justice, which means a man must be punished. She wants space that could be taken by a man. Are we really willing to make that sacrifice?

What makes a woman's ambition predatory, we are told, is that it overflows its natural bounds. It treads on the lands men have marked as theirs: all political power, all financial power, all right to the upper echelons of literature and art. All control over what happens to women's bodies, finances, futures. The Harpy aspires to what does not belong to her—which, when nothing is granted, is the same as saying she aspires at all. The allowable territory grows and shrinks with time: once it would have been unthinkable for women to aim for a job at all, let alone a job running a country. But wherever we draw the line for women, it becomes the fixed point between the reasonable and the grotesque. On one side, the things we're allowed to ask for: the crumbs men have designated for our use. On the other side, everything else, which is rightfully theirs.

❧

While I was writing this, the *Huffington Post* ran a story headlined "Vomiting Vultures Completely Take Over Couple's Luxury Vacation Home." Response to the publication's evocative tweet—"Dozens of vomiting and defecating black vultures have overtaken a New York couple's luxury Florida vacation house, tearing up screens and attacking cars with their beaks"—was swift and delighted, hundreds of people rooting for the birds. The image of rapacious winged creatures befouling ill-gotten gains, so troubling to Virgil, became downright inspirational once the victim was a country club home mere miles from Mar-a-Lago. Twitter, in 2019, was wise to how wealth works: you may "own" vacation property, but probably just because you stole from someone else somewhere down the line. If a vulture shits on it, well, that's praxis.

The owners of the home, I imagine, would have objected: that's their house, bought with their money, and no vulture has the right to vomit all over it. But leftist Twitter has enthusiastically embraced the idea that property is theft, or anyway that wealth derives from exploitation. And besides, who has a longer ancestral claim to the Florida wetlands: a flock of vultures or a couple of snowbirds?

All these Twitter leftists instinctively grasped "vultures are not stealing from rich people." "Women are not stealing recognition or praise or sex from men" seems to present more of a challenge. But it's a difference of degree more than kind: in both cases, the point is that people (or birds) can't steal what you don't really own. You can designate power and achievement as your natural property, and argue on that basis that you are their landlord and sole rightful tenant, but that means about as much in reality as a deed means to a vulture.

The fear of the snatcher, whether it's the Harpy coming for your food or the woman coming for your political seat or the vultures coming for your vacation home, depends on the conviction that everything you have is your dominion and your due. But what if recognition, power, talent, influence are not foreign domains where women need permission to step? What if it's not arrogance to dominate our professional fields, our areas of expertise, our own bodies? What if the cattle had belonged to Celaeno and her sisters all along?

These territories are not owned by men. We are not trespassers here.

THAT'S WHAT
YOU THINK

W HEN I WAS IN MY EARLY TWENTIES, I lived in Dupont Circle in Washington, DC. A few blocks south lived the man I thought I was in love with. (That's not why I lived in Dupont—there aren't that many cool places to live in DC—but it also wasn't *not* why.) Halfway between us was a Masonic temple, its door flanked by twin sphinxes twice my height.

When you think of a sphinx, you may immediately picture the one guarding the Great Pyramid of Giza: a lion's body and an impassive human face with headdress. Egyptian sphinxes are probably male, though there's no real guarantee (the Great Sphinx of Giza weighs thousands of tons; nobody has flipped it over to check). The sphinxes at the Masonic temple are Egyptian-influenced sphinxes, down to the hieroglyphics on their breastplates, but they could be as plausibly women as men: broad, high-cheekboned faces, neither fine nor rough of feature, and elaborately braided hair. They're known as the Sphinx of Wisdom and the Sphinx of Power. Power has its eyes open, looking outward. Wisdom has its eyes half-closed, looking inside.

I never went inside the temple, but I walked past it often, and every time I took a certain kind of comfort in the statues' impassive, androgynous faces. I had a strong preference for Wisdom, which looks beatific: its expression softer, its features a touch more feminine. I've always been a little frightened of oversized statues; just a mile away was the Dumbarton

Bridge, known locally as Buffalo Bridge, whose looming bison statues scared me so much that I kept my eyes locked on the ground when crossing it. But climbing the temple's wide, shallow steps to sit beneath Wisdom felt like a tolerable kind of fear, even a healthy one—a grounding fear. Power, with its staring, pupilless eyes, was less of a comfort.

If I'd been wiser at the time, I might have realized that this is because power is dangerous. I wasn't wiser yet.

Unlike the Egyptian sphinx, which is a category of creature, there is only one Sphinx in Greek myth. She, like the sphinxes on the Masonic temple, has a lion's body and a human head, but she also tends to be depicted with unmistakably feminine breasts. (In the version of Ingres's *Oedipus and the Sphinx* painting that's at the Walters Art Museum in Baltimore, she's almost nothing else. Her breasts glow out of the shadows of the cave she sits in, which hide her wings and lion haunches and face.) Artistic depictions often feminize her in other ways too. Although she has the body of a lion, it's as if artists couldn't bring themselves to give her a lion's power. In the Ingres painting, she's closer to the size of a cheetah. In Gustave Moreau's *Oedipus and the Sphinx*, she clings to Oedipus's chest like a large angry kitten. Ancient carvings, too, are frequently closer to cats than lions. (The masculine Giza Sphinx, by contrast, is 240 feet long.)

These are all male artists I'm talking about, of course. The best-known version of the Sphinx's story is by a man too: Sophocles, in his play *Oedipus Rex*. Men have clamored for hundreds of years to diminish the Sphinx, to show her as small and surmountable. The story of the Sphinx is the story of a woman with questions men can't answer. Men didn't take that any better in the fifth century BCE than they do now.

Here's how Sophocles tells it. The Sphinx traveled to Thebes from foreign lands and menaced the city, devouring anyone who couldn't answer her riddle: What goes on four legs in the morning, two in the evening, and three at night? The answer was "man," who crawls as a baby, walks upright as an adult, and later leans on a cane. The wording of the riddle varies a little in different tellings and translations, but it's always something along these lines, and go figure, the answer is always "man." Anyway, the king of Thebes offered rule of the city—and the hand of Jocasta, widow of the king's son Laius—to anyone who could rid him of this scourge. Oedipus, the prince of a neighboring city, answered the riddle, took the throne, and wed Jocasta. The Sphinx, defeated, threw herself to her death.

Oedipus naturally thought he was pretty smart after this. What he didn't know, though, was that at birth he had been prophesied to kill his father and marry his mother. His frightened father had left him outside Thebes to die, but instead he was taken in by the childless rulers of nearby Corinth. That father was Laius, and his mother was Jocasta. Hot-headed Oedipus had dispatched with Laius, unknown to him, after a quarrel on the road on his way to Thebes. By defeating the Sphinx and marrying Jocasta, he completed the prophecy.

Oedipus did not save Thebes by defeating the Sphinx. In fact, he doomed it. A pestilence settled over the city, divine punishment for its king and queen's incestuous marriage. But he did at least save it from this specific threat: the monster and her mystery. He showed the Sphinx's great mysterious heart to be something mundane, a child's riddle with a solution so commonplace you could have stumbled on the answer by just naming things you see. He bested her so thoroughly that she made herself disappear.

There are other ways, though, to tell this story. Mid-twentieth-century American feminist poet Muriel Rukeyser, for instance, has a poem about Oedipus's encounter with the Sphinx, called "Myth." In her retelling, a blinded Oedipus encounters the Sphinx again, and asks her why he didn't recognize his mother. The Sphinx tells him that his answer was wrong all along—he said man, but he never said woman:

"When you say Man," said Oedipus, "you include women too.
Everyone knows that."   She said, "That's what
you think."

The terror of the Sphinx is the terror of a woman holding secrets from men, posing puzzles that men can't solve. It's the terror of a woman saying, "That's what *you* think," because she knows something more. The narratives given to female monsters, by male playwrights and poets and authors, are often allegories: *This is what happens to the woman who oversteps, who breaks the boundaries.* In this case, the myth sets up a woman of fearsome power, but the story exists to bring her down, to sweep her away from the center of her own tale. To take the secrets of women and make men the key. It's a way of punishing her for knowing too much, for making men look like fools: men put themselves at the center of the story, at the center of the riddle of the Sphinx.

The Sphinx, the story goes, held occult knowledge inaccessible to men, until a man knew the answer. Until a man *was* the answer. And then, leached of her one secret, she dashed herself on the rocks, and the man won—and although his ignorance was still his downfall, at least there was no monstrous woman who knew more. That's the only story of the Sphinx.

That's what you think.

⟍⟋

This man I thought I was in love with did not love me back, which is already a kind of power if you're prepared to exploit it; people will debase themselves so much for love. Add to this the fact that when we met, he was my professor. I had needed a break from my hothouse women's college, so I took a year off, and then did my senior year somewhere else. This meant that after a full school career being younger than anyone else in my grade, I had finally caught up. I was twenty-one when I started his class, living off campus with my much older boyfriend, more focused and pragmatic about school than I had been before my hiatus. I thought that meant I was mature enough to invite my cute teacher to poker night, and then agree to a weekly study date, and then start helping him shop for clothes and kitchenware, and then tell him I had a crush on him, and then act on the crush, all before finishing my senior year. (I broke up with the boyfriend somewhere in there, but not early enough.) I wasn't, in fact, mature enough for any of those things, but then I wasn't mature enough to know that.

What I was, though, was eager to please, and he was eager to let me. He was not going to love me, but he did want someone to massage his back and give him a ride to IKEA and clean his apartment and stroke his ego and suck his dick. He wanted someone to provide him with a ready-made group of friends he could analyze behind their backs. He wanted someone to help him shop for furniture and clothes, to memorize his preferences and carry his bags—we did a lot of that, even early on, leaving separately from campus to the mall so nobody would see. It was worth it, because sometimes he would wear sweaters or shoes we bought together to class, and I would think *that was me. I did that.* To me, it was a message about my importance. Being useful was the closest I could come to feeling desired. To him, they were just his clothes. (Once another student remarked, "He dresses so young, it's weirdly hot." Huh, I said. Does he? Is it?)

I don't mean to suggest that he was exploiting me consciously. I'm sure he *liked* me, in the particular way you like people who make you feel good. (From my diary, or rather from the scattered email drafts and private LiveJournal posts that served as a diary at the time: *He has been touching me in public, lately.*) But he never let me forget that he didn't love me, and worse, he always made it seem as if he *could*—if I could be more deserving, quicker to correct myself, less likely to test him, more obedient, less needy. He never said there would be a reward if I completed those assignments. But how could there not be? I was trying so hard.

(From my diary: *If I can stay silent for four days, he will be happy to hear from me on the fifth.*)

(From my diary: *Being useful makes me more tolerable.* When I helped him move apartments, a multiday affair, he let me stay over twice in a row, an unprecedented occurrence. All I had to do was pack during the nights and carry during the days.)

"I really do want you to be happy," he told me once. "I just need you to put in some effort."

"But all I do is try to make *you* happy," I protested.

He sighed. "When you say things like that, it forces me to either be obliged to you or use you blatantly. You know I don't want to play that kind of game."

It's difficult to explain what made it so bad, because I am so well-trained now to doubt myself. There is a sort of double consciousness in looking back on those days, a woozy judder to the outlines, like looking at a 3D picture without the glasses. If I start to describe some specific cause of friction—the time I told him it was raining and he was angry because he already knew, the time I sent a Wikipedia link to settle a dispute in my favor, all the times I told him my feelings were hurt and he disagreed—it falls apart in my hands. Surely he can't have been *that* mad about one little correction, and maybe I *did* intend to gloat over being right about the difference between moss and lichen, and anyway he never yelled; shouldn't I have thanked him for not yelling, for not being more cruel when he could have been? (Actually, I did. From my emails: *I know there were a number of times last night when you were not as hurtful as you could be, and as you pointed out the hurtful path is sometimes easiest, so thanks for that.*) It rang true when he said I only told him my feelings in order to blame or manipulate him—I wanted so much from him, and he was so uninterested in my stupid little heartbreaks, so what other reason could there be? Maybe I really was mentally ill, like he said, or suffering brain damage from childhood stress—he was the expert, after all. And certainly he was right that I was self-obsessed and talked about myself all the time, or how would I know so many things he thought about me?

(From my diary: *I'm sick of him controlling all our interactions and I'm sick of him telling me what I think. It's not like he's my boyfriend. He shouldn't be allowed to dictate my behavior like this.* Also from my diary: *He's justified in wanting me to be as bearable as possible. He probably doesn't* want *to have to tell me all the things that are wrong with me.*)

Would I have doubted myself without his help? Of course I would. Very young women are exquisite machines of self-doubt, and machinists too: always innovating, always tinkering, finding new ways to weld together the judgments of our parents and peers and strangers into a perpetual motion device. He didn't build that engine; he only stoked it. But he stoked it frequently, and unpredictably, and often just when I had started to find my feet—and no matter how unfair it felt, he was always right, because he had to be. Was I in his class when I first read about Martin

Seligman's learned helplessness experiments, where he shocked his canine subjects no matter how they behaved until they were reduced to cowering, sniveling beasts? I identified so much with those dogs.

There is nothing unusual about the story of a young woman turning herself inside out for a man in a position of authority. It's a cliché, the kind of thing old white male writers structure novels around when they're too established to need to be creative. At the time, though, it felt intensely personal, a daily referendum on my specific insufficiencies. It was like the moment right before someone breaks up with you, and the moment after, repeated on a loop for years: the vertiginous nausea of rejection, the willingness to do anything, believe anything, accept anything, ask nothing. A permanent home in the bargaining phase of grief. I kept mental lists of the clothes and colors he favored, the foods he preferred, how he liked his back rubbed and hair washed. I cleaned his apartment for him, in the nude if he asked me to. I tinkered with formulas for figuring out how often I could ask for his attention before my existence became a burden and he was forced to remind me, again, that I was beneath him. I was, at all times, building a sort of Rosetta stone for translating his needs into something I could make use of: a code for how to make myself indispensable. It never worked. I was translating from a language I was not meant to understand.

(From my diary: *He likes panang curry, but with some vegetables, not all tofu. He likes Boddingtons Ale and good frozen margaritas and thinks Kashi cereal is magic. He likes bedding in lava colors like dark red and grey. If he's wearing a particular pair of pants, eating cellophane noodles, or drinking tea, he's sick; if he rubs his head in a certain way he has a headache. His spine is bent 17 degrees to the right side. He doesn't like lit candles on the table. When you're shampooing his hair you ought to dig your fingers in head-massage-style. He can't blow his nose. He washes his clothes on the gentle cycle with Woolite, black pants inside out, and dries them on a rack. Bananas hurt his mouth. He doesn't like dark nipples, ribs, or skinny legs, but he doesn't mind breast implants if they're done right. He likes his porn to have a plot. He likes popping bubble wrap. He never meant for me to be remembering all this shit.*)

This is, again, not rare. It's expected. Recommended, even. Very young women are supposed to expose our underbellies to older men who will tell us how to improve—and improving is, of course, supposed to mean making ourselves useful. When it comes to the stories that shape our social consciousness, there is nothing unnatural about this tableau: a young woman on her literal and figurative knees in front of a more powerful, wiser male figure. This is Jane Eyre and Rochester, Dorothea and Casaubon, Bella and Edward, every student-professor liaison in every work of literary fiction I've ever refused to read. I was only able to slot myself so neatly into this narrative because there was a space carved out explicitly for me.

But it always chafed. I tried to be the clean vessel I was supposed to be, the one he had room for: useful and undemanding, a piece of storage. On those sun-glazed marble stairs under the sphinxes, halfway between our houses, I tried over and over to empty myself out. But all the time, Wisdom and Power were whispering: *This isn't the only story. This is not the story for you.*

The Sphinx is doubly othered: her form, though not her name or her story, came over to Greece from Egypt, and Greek accounts retain her foreign origins. She is sent into Thebes by a vengeful god, from elsewhere, bearing a maddeningly opaque secret. She thus taps into anxieties about the intelligence of women and of outsiders. In the society I grew up in, these fears—and the privilege-protective lies they generate—manifest in slightly different ways: nonwhite people and immigrants are implied to be intellectually inferior because they are closer to animals, women because they are closer to children. These slanders are related in the way they cast the Other's intelligence as incomplete—sometimes atavistic, sometimes immature, but in any case, stunted. And they are related in the deep-seated disquiet they protect: the dominant party's fear that the Other may not only be equal in intelligence but have intuition or judgment or arcane knowledge that penetrates all his protective bluster and sees to his rotten, weak heart.

We don't enshrine the idea of the inferior Other into culture because we think it's true. (I say "we" here because I'm partially culpable. I may not be a man, but that doesn't mean I'm never a patriarchal villain.) Certainly there are people simple and scared enough to believe the line they're sold, that anyone different is lesser, but that's not why the story's for sale in the first place. It's for sale because it's a comforting lie, a salve for the fear—for the knowledge—that men and white people and Westerners and the wealthy win because we cheat. We have raised up these self-serving falsehoods as a fortress against the fear, a way to kneecap any marginalized group's attempt to take the dominant parties down. There is nobody more delicate, after all, than the person who has set himself up to win without a fight.

This is why we tell ourselves fairy tales about the IQ bell curve, as though it means anything to ace a test when you're the one who wrote the questions. This is why we have tropes like the Magical Negro and the Manic Pixie Dream Girl, so even those Others whose special skills and insights are acknowledged must be seen putting them to use for the good of the white male hero. This is also why we normalize, even valorize, the idea of the naive young woman and the authoritative man. If you set things up so the Other has no chance to challenge you—because she can't get a foothold, because the rules won't let her win, because she lacks the experience or resources or advancement that you've granted yourself—then your position stays secure.

The Sphinx breaks these bulwarks in two with her lion's claws. Her power is seeing beyond the stories allowed to her, with their paltry linear paths. Her view is broader, a perspective from the zenith of wisdom, all possibilities and connections and syntheses arcing out like fireworks. She will not give up or diminish her stores of wisdom for anyone's comfort; she will not pretend to know less than she does. She is a keeper of secrets, a holder of knowledge, and that knowledge is for herself. Yes, a man cracks her code, yes, a man is the answer—but only in the easy story, the story we've been handed, the story mediated by men who want to be more than they are. The Sphinx, the monster of knowledge, is larger than the cautionary tale men have trapped her in.

Men do not like for women to outdo them. Some of them will lie to keep from being outdone. Some will hurt you. Some will find you young and keep you small. And some of them will trap you in a story like a cage: a story where only he can crack your riddle, a story where he is a savior just for knowing more than you.

It's easy to get stuck in that story. It's the story that has a space for you, the story that welcomes you in; to escape it means turning the whole world upside down. The girl is supposed to be young and ductile, eager to please and easily led. The monster isn't supposed to know more than the hero. This is how stories work.

That's what you think.

❧

Usually, when monsters of antiquity are vanquished, what this means is that they're killed by the conquering hero. In rare cases, they may simply be captured or tamed. But only the Sphinx is intellectually overpowered until she vanquishes herself.

To me, this self-defeat reads as a punishment: an indignity visited on the Sphinx by male authors for her secretiveness and her pride. She is literally knocked from the pedestal she's sitting on. Knowledge, in and of itself, is not out of reach for female heroes, as long as it is ultimately used for the good of a man: Hermione leveraging her superior schooling and skill to get Harry Potter out of a jam. But the Sphinx hoards her knowledge—taunts men with it, even. Forces them to face their ignorance. Of course the narrative can't stop at merely having her physically bested; that doesn't kill the secrets, or the shame. She has to be humiliated, her secrets blown open, and having been debased she has to undermine herself. To defeat a monstrous mind, you must start from inside.

In real life, this works fearsomely well. If you can set up someone's story this way—knowledge as an unconscionable act of hubris, hubris as a self-immolating sin—it might take them lifetimes to learn to tell another. Everything they think they know, after all, becomes suspect, the simple act of claiming authority enough to trigger a defeatist leap. *Was it all my fault? Was what he said really so devastating? Was he actually right all along?*

The threat of the Sphinx is the threat of a woman, an Other, with inaccessible depths, with undisclosed insights. The fantasy of the Sphinx is the fantasy that this monstrous woman will not only be destroyed, but will destroy herself, systematically—that she will not only lose her position of power but renounce it. It's a fantasy of petty revenge.

It doesn't have to happen that way, of course. But my god, will they try.

❧

An infant Sphinx must look like a baby-faced kitten, soft claws and blunt little human milk teeth. It must seem like the kind of creature you can toy with and tease and even torment—but that only works as long as it never grows. And you can't keep it from growing forever, no matter how powerful its adolescent weakness makes you feel.

Trying to disentangle myself was an endless process, not least because I didn't really want to. I would go to his house intending to cut things off, and wind up sleeping over—well, not *over*, since he always woke me and sent me out woozy in the middle of the night, but certainly not leaving when I should. In the morning, I wouldn't be able to reconstruct the conversation. (From my diary: *I don't know what happened through a lot of it—why was I crying? How did he end up reiterating that he didn't love me and why, even when I asked that he not tell me again? How did I manage to botch this so bad?*) It helped that I went to graduate school, where I had other people to impress. It helped that I got new friends who didn't mock me as much, friends I hadn't even told him much about because he always said I only spoke fondly of others in order to insult him by comparison. It helped that I slept with other people, and eventually got a new boyfriend. But it didn't help enough.

Fortunately, when I was twenty-five, he moved out of the country, and it was out of my hands. On his last night, he wanted me to come over and help him pack. A year earlier, I would have canceled everything for the chance to stay up all night doing his work for him; I would have told myself it was what I wanted. But I had plans with my boyfriend and the new friends he didn't know. I had told him I would come over the previous day, but I didn't, because he never called. I'd only seen him at his goodbye dinner, which he said didn't count because our other friends were there. (What did he think I, a person with a boyfriend, was going to do for him that I couldn't do in front of them? He was probably right.) Anyway, he said, I owed it to him to come over immediately, because I'd promised months ago I would sew a button onto something for him. I said I'd forgotten, and he said, "That's because it involves you doing something for somebody else." Then he claimed he was kidding. I didn't go. He didn't talk to me again for a year.

The next—almost the last—time I heard from him, he explained his silence by saying he didn't trust me anymore. He didn't say what he didn't trust me to *do*, but these days, I can fill that in myself: he didn't trust me to drop everything and come when he called. He didn't trust me to doubt myself, to throw away my understanding of who I was, of what had happened between us, and substitute the one he offered me. He didn't trust me never to deny him. He was almost right about that too. He was so close to being right.

But instead he stopped trusting me, and then he disappeared. And I stopped being quite so young, at more or less the usual rate. While I never entirely learned to trust *myself*—I always thought he might have had my number all along, that I was ungrateful and selfish and smug and passive-aggressive and crazy to boot, and that there was no clearer proof of this than my endless and futile attempts to do exactly what he wanted—I got better at it the longer he was away. I didn't stop hearing his voice in my head, and sometimes, to my horror, coming out of my mouth: a phrase he would have used, or a cruel thing he would have said about my selfishness and ingratitude, delivered as a fact. But it happened less and less.

And then, thirteen years to the day after he left, he emailed me again.

❧

I couldn't do more than skim the email at first. The effect of seeing his name in my inbox—or inboxes, because he also sent it to my work—was too immediately physical: nausea, hyperventilation, tears, and then an immediate wave of self-recrimination for overreacting so badly. Before the panic had ebbed, I was already doubting its validity; even his virtual presence started to fray my ability to trust that I know what I feel. (If I'd told him I wanted to throw up, what would he say? That I didn't? That I was only saying that to insult him? Would he be right?) Other people's responses when I told them, which ranged from "oh god I'm so sorry" to "I will murder him," seemed to support my recollections and my response, but I'd immediately lost my grip on any kind of internal barometer. If he could write me a breezy, mildly chummy message with no hint of resentment or apology, did that mean I'd been overburdening the entire relationship, blaming him unfairly for the darkness and desolation of those years?

And it *was* a breezy message, as I discovered once I'd had a Klonopin and lifted some weights and sent half a dozen frantic texts. He had seen some boots he thought I'd like. (I didn't.) My writing was very good, as I probably already knew. (I did.) He would love to get back in touch, if I was interested. (I wasn't.)

(I wasn't. Was I?) (Was I?)

(I *didn't* like the boots, right? I *had* already known my work was good?)

I had become so accustomed to undermining myself at his urging that his lightest touch made me doubt everything: my panic, my instinctive revulsion, my memories of what happened between us and the framework I used to understand them. Faced with his reappearance, something I'd dreamed or daydreamed often (sometimes as reconciliation, often as vengeance, rarely as apology; even in dreams, I wasn't stupid), it was hard even to trust reality. After the 2016 election, I was already prone to viewing the world as a malign alternate dimension, and the whole thing just seemed so *implausible*, so calculated specifically to throw me into a spin. I plucked at fantasies about brains in jars and cruel simulation programmers, *Matrix*-style. (Thirteen years *to the day!* It strains credulity! I didn't realize that part until much later, of course, but it added to the air of unreality surrounding the whole event.) I checked my trash folders daily to be sure I hadn't made it all up. It was like a concussion: the warped 3D-glasses outlines back on everything, the reality I knew layered over again with the one he wanted me to see, the version where it was perfectly normal for him to email me about some shoes because he'd never damaged me beyond repair.

What was stranger, although no more welcome, was that he now seemed to see me as an equal—he called me an "old friend." (I wasn't.) He expressed admiration for the "transformation" he saw evidenced in my writing, as if I had experienced some kind of miraculous personal renaissance. Once I started to feel angry, this was the part I felt angry about: the way he tried to pin me in place with his praise. Of course I had changed, the way anyone would in thirteen years, but I hadn't "transformed"; I'd just grown up. The version of me he knew had been tender and stunted—tender from actual youth and inexperience (my brain hadn't even finished developing, as he well knew!), and stunted by having someone tell me over and over that I was wrong about what I felt, wrong about what I thought, wrong about what I wanted, hoping to watch me dash myself on the rocks for aiming too high.

Men employ so many tricks to let themselves stay intellectually superior. The cultural valorizing of female youth is only one of the shortcuts, a way for men to seamlessly surround themselves with women who aren't yet fully equipped to challenge them. There's also the historical barring of women from education or advancement. There's taking credit for women's ideas, or parroting her own jokes back to her. There's dismissing her knowledge as lesser or flawed because it comes from her. And when all else fails, there's the Sphinx option: drive her to undermine herself.

What does the Sphinx look like outside of these manipulations and tricks? What does she look like outside of the stories where "man" is the answer, the stories men tell about her? Grown and glossy, blood in her paws, bodies in her wake, wings like a carven arch against the sky: a monster of pure knowledge, the true queen of Thebes. Men may build all the stories they like to try to take her secrets from her, to try to take back the kingdom they believe was theirs to begin with. Let them try. Before she fishes their heart out with a claw, she purrs: *That's what you think.*

❦

Even in death the Sphinx is blamed for continuing to devastate the city. Oedipus punctures her riddle, drives her to self-destruction, puts her in her place, then takes the wife and throne he's earned in the process—but the kingdom he now reigns over is struck by drought and disease. "That pest which I destroyed is now destroying Thebes," he complains in Seneca's version of the tragedy. From where Oedipus stands, the story has only one monster. Once she's vanquished, if the curse persists, the fault must be with her ghost.

The reader knows why it really happened, of course—why the gods are punishing the city that Oedipus rules alongside Jocasta. The story of Oedipus relies on dramatic irony: a device in which the audience knows something crucial that a character does not know. We watch Oedipus hurtle towards his incestuous marriage, thinking he's being a hero. We watch the gods punish him and his city for his deeds. And what tale would the Sphinx tell? How many untold stories does she hold? If she knows the riddle that makes everything possible, what else must she know?

The riddle of man is answered, and she's made to suffer for it, but there's no version of the tale that promises the Sphinx had only one secret. Oedipus fails abjectly in the end, felled by the part of the myth he didn't know. If she had lived, if she had owned the story, who knows who else the Sphinx might have brought down. Great and terrible she is, unshackled by the narratives built to restrain her.

Part of me feels that I shouldn't do this man the honor of writing about him. Why give him the satisfaction? If he's suddenly such a fan of my work, why give him the reflected light? To tell someone the ways they wrecked your life, you have to tell them they're important. Some people don't need to hear that message again.

But then again, I'm the only one in charge of the story now. I get to tell you what he wanted, what he thought, what kind of person he was—what kind of person he is now, even, based on the kind of person who emails lovers from over a decade ago. It's a terrible way to behave, painting this man in such a negative light without giving him the opportunity to contradict me again. A great and terrible way to behave.

❧

Oedipus proved himself to be a certain kind of smart, a certain kind of wise: a lateral thinker, sure, a person not bound by the mental shackles of literalism. A person capable of realizing that a story that doesn't seem to be about him is about him after all. But the Sphinx is monstrously smart, monstrously wise. Of course her answer wouldn't be simple; of course it would have layers, locks within locks. Oedipus's answer, the answer that does not see women, is what wins him Jocasta's hand in marriage, dooming him and her and Thebes. Why would that solution, the answer of a man obsessed with himself, open the right door?

This is the Sphinx I believe in: Rukeyser's Sphinx, the one who has been in charge of the story all along. The one who always knew that the simple answer to her riddle was the wrong one. And this is, of course, the Oedipus I believe in too: old and shamed and blinded by his own hubris, still telling a woman who knows more than him what everyone knows. Still expecting her to leap to her death out of shame for hoarding her secrets.

Too late to expect that. The Sphinx is ready to rise back to her pedestal, to ask her second riddle: the question Oedipus was never asked. (The version of the story with two riddles appears, as far as I can tell, only in Theodectes's version of *Oedipus*, a century after Sophocles, and even that, we only know about secondhand. But the Sphinx breaks the boundaries of story, takes what she likes.) The second riddle is this: There are two sisters, one of whom births the other, while the second gives birth to the first. The answer is night and day, both feminine words in Greek—but it could just as easily be the female hero and the female monster. A mutual parthenogenesis of two archetypes who, without the gaze of a man, aren't so different at all. That's not the only private untouched knowledge we hold, but it's one of our secrets: that without the cowardly and powerful making her into a threat, the monster is the mother and child of the hero. We don't ask them that riddle. They wouldn't understand the answer, and we don't want them to.

Those in power will always set themselves up to stay in power; they will write the questions so that the answers are the ones they know. They'll call knowledge that isn't made for them "unscientific" or "occult"—look at the newly self-anointed medieval doctors calling women's healing "witchcraft," and healing that barred women "medicine." They'll tell stories where that knowledge is punished, or diminished, or warped to fit their needs, or simply filtered through their contempt. They'll keep the people around them ignorant or young or small, so they will not be challenged, so if challenged, they can always win. They'll expect to see the Sphinx dash herself on the rocks.

They'll forget she has wings.

SOCIAL JUSTICE WARRIORS

ONE OF MY FAVORITE pieces of writing in the world is the appendix of the book *The Sting of the Wild* by entomologist Justin Schmidt. Here, on his bespoke sting pain scale, Schmidt catalogs various insect bites he has suffered over the course of his career. His pain scale reads more like a list of perfumes or wines. The wasp section, for instance, ranges from level-0.5 pain like the potter wasp ("Rich and full-bodied in appearance but flavorless") through level 2 like the western yellowjacket ("Hot and smoky, almost irreverent") to the rare level 4 like the warrior wasp ("Torture. You are chained in the flow of an active volcano. Why did I start this list?"). There's so much exquisite variety to pain, when carefully observed. For most people, the stings of the artistic wasp, the honey wasp, the fierce black polybia wasp, and the unstable paper wasp—all real insects with stings clocking in at 2 on the four-point scale—would blend together under the heading "Fucking Ow!" But for Justin Schmidt, who has made enough peace with his pain to view it from the outside, subtleties and gradations appear: one sting is spicy, another droning, a third abstract ("Love and marriage followed by divorce").

I have been thinking about the sting pain scale a lot over the last few years. Unpleasant experiences that used to be rare enough to need no categorization are now so common that we're starting to notice the finer gradations, the different subtle textures of anger and outrage and fear. It's not only that the world has gotten worse, although it has; the future has contracted painfully, shorter and uglier now than it's ever been. It's also that the internet makes us chaotically, catastrophically aware at every minute of how bad the world is and how bad it's going to get. We are adrift in an ocean of anger, or maybe we are adrift in terror and anger is the flotsam we cling to. Or maybe anger is both the ocean and the raft. Anyway, we are drowning.

This is what makes me think about the classification of sting pain: the sting of insects, the sting of fear, the sting of anger. How do you cope with a day that might include a guy catcalling you on your commute *and* a murderous cop going free *and* a nationwide attack on reproductive rights—*and* an army of Twitter trolls telling you that all of this is good, actually, and anti-fascism is the real fascism? *And* the knowledge, churning under it all, that the government is corrupt and the country is built on white supremacy and the planet has thirty years and nobody is doing anything? You either let it all wash over you together, a tsunami ready to pull you under, or you stand outside the pain and watch.

What would an anger index look like, if women cataloged our thousand daily ires? There's the irritation of having your space impinged on by an oblivious manspreader: a prickly flush, like a sunburn. The exasperation of being left to arrange all the details, as always, because it's assumed you will: hard but voltaic, like biting into a brick of tin foil. The resentment of watching white men fail upward with no cognizance of their own relative worth, or demand special treatment because it's what they've become accustomed to: a volcanic heat in the scalp, a crown of red-hot iron. The enormity of remembering the president has been credibly accused of rape by more than a dozen women with no perceptible political consequences: like food poisoning in an important meeting.

And then there's fury.

What does fury feel like? Does it feel like a snake wrapped around your body? Does it feel like poison on your breath?

The Furies, the monster-goddesses of vengeance, bristle with snakes—snakes in their hair, wreathing their limbs, fastening their garments, held in their hands like whips. Snakes, in the symbolism of Greek mythology, often marked creatures as "chthonic," associated with the underworld, and that's true here. In Ovid's version, the Furies are the guards of souls deemed too wicked for paradise. Other storytellers make them not just guards, but judges; they can damn you for eternity, or drag you down to hell themselves. In Homer, they are curses made flesh, sicced on those who commit a crime or threaten the natural order. Seneca the Younger calls them "they who with awful brows investigate men's crimes and sift out ancient wrongs." They wear black or blood red, sometimes dripping with actual blood; their eyes are steely, and they breathe out poisonous fumes.

Despite all this, the blood and the snakes and the black robes covered in gore, the Furies are often called the Eumenides: the Kindly Ones. Like calling fairies "the fair folk," this pseudonym is part dodge, part puffery. The hope is that if you call them by a flattering nickname, they won't notice you're talking about them, or if they do, perhaps they won't hurt you. (The word "euphemism" and Eumenides share a root: *eu-*, for "good.") Their real names are Tisiphone, Alecto, and Megaera: Avenger of Murder, Unceasing Anger, and Jealousy.

The word "fury," as we use it today, implies a chaotic, unfocused frenzy of rage. But the Furies embodied *justified* anger, stemming from an adamantine moral code. They look fearsome, and they are; anger with reason and purpose and a will of iron is even more threatening than tumultuous, flailing rage if you're the one in the crosshairs. But they're fearsome like a sniper, focused and specific. They hunt down the wicked and punish them, both in life and after death. The wrath of the Furies is not capricious. It's directed at matricides and fratricides, perjurers, oathbreakers, and those who offend the gods. It is targeted and implacable, the striking hand of a finely tuned clockwork structure of morals and values.

So maybe the Furies are kind after all. They're for sure not *nice*—but niceness is often the opposite of justice. Niceness encourages you to make exceptions, to keep quiet, to smooth things over, to think of that boy's bright future. As any number of inspirational websites hasten to remind us, though, "kind" is not the same as "nice." The name "Kindly Ones" elides this difference—to me, at least, "kindly" conjures up the image of Prince Humperdinck's father in *The Princess Bride*, patting Buttercup's arm and saying "That's nice, dear" when she says she'll be dead by morning. But in Greek, *Eumenides* means something closer to "the righteous ones"—the ones who are inflamed with the desire to do good. And righteousness without kindness is zealotry.

Aeschylus's play *The Eumenides*, in which the titular goddesses seek vengeance on Orestes, prince of Mycenae, makes clear the deeply principled nature of their wrath. Aeschylus has no love for the Furies; many of his characters really go hog-wild describing how gross, old, and smelly they are. The plot of the play confounds, contradicts, and ultimately humiliates them, but even Aeschylus still portrays them as stubbornly ethical, unwavering in their commitment to their ideals.

Orestes was the son of Agamemnon, who commanded the Greek forces during the Trojan War. By the time Agamemnon returned home from Troy, he had a concubine in tow and his wife, Clytemnestra, had taken a lover, Aegisthus. Either Clytemnestra or Aegisthus, depending on the story you choose, murdered Agamemnon in his bath. In retribution—the Greek tragedies are a flurry of retribution—Orestes arranged to murder Clytemnestra and her man. This is what brings down the Furies, punishers of (among other things) matricide. They doggedly pursue Orestes from Argos to Delphi to Athens, seeking to punish him for murdering his mother.

But the play, for the most part, isn't a chase scene. It's a court procedural. (It is, in fact, about the *invention* of court procedure, about the modern-style trial system replacing instinctive bloody revenge.) When it opens, the Furies have run Orestes to ground; then some protective gods show up, and the majority of the play is taken up with a lengthy debate about whether Orestes should be held responsible for Clytemnestra's death. A legal battle could not possibly be less like a violent frenzy, but the Furies—even though they symbolize, within the play, an outdated mode of vengeance—duly plead their case and agree to abide by the outcome. Their goal, after all, is not merely blood. It is justice.

What makes women's anger monstrous? As with hunger and brilliance and ambition, it's partly just the overstepping of closely guarded bounds. There will always be only so much emotion a woman, even a supposedly powerful woman, is allowed to have. Anger in particular is more stingily restricted the darker you are. The perennially restrained Michelle Obama was dogged by accusations of outsized anger for her eight years in the White House and beyond, simply because she was female and black and, very gently, nobody's fool.

But women's anger is particularly reviled when it is nocked and aimed, the sharp end of an unwavering system of beliefs about what we will not endure. A Fury's anger. Men fear our chaotic rage, but not nearly as much as they fear our focused grievances about very real injustice. There is little more threatening to the social order than a woman who's angry. The only thing scarier is a woman who's angry *about* something. The only thing scarier than that is a woman who's right.

A 2015 study from Arizona State University, which looked at gender bias in a simulated jury deliberation, found that men were deemed more credible when they spoke with heat while women expressing anger made the people around them stubborn and resistant. Subjects participated in a mock trial in which they had to agree with other "jurors"—purportedly other study participants but actually creations of the researchers—on whether to convict. Through messages, four of the five fictional jurors would agree with whatever verdict the participant settled on. The remaining one—the only juror given a gender-coded name—would disagree. This holdout might express his or her dissenting opinion with anger, with fear, or in a neutral tone. When the holdout's name sounded like a man's, and he spoke with passion, subjects were often swayed. When the holdout's name sounded like a woman's, they doubled down on their original opinion. Or, in academic-ese: "Participants' confidence in their own verdict dropped significantly after male holdouts expressed anger. Participants became significantly more confident in their original verdicts after female holdouts expressed anger, even though they were expressing the exact same opinion and emotion as the male holdouts."

"What is most disturbing about the findings is that they were produced by anger, specifically," said the study's coauthor Jessica Salerno in a press release. "If you think about when we express anger, it is often when we really care about something, when we are most passionate and most convicted about a decision. Our results suggest that gender gaps in influence are most likely to materialize in these situations—when we are arguing for something we care about most."

This same instinct—to fear and denigrate women's anger specifically when it comes from principle—is behind the absurd online insult "Social Justice Warrior." This supposed taunt, levied not exclusively but especially at women who stand up for progressive principles, accidentally sounds cool as hell. It's not the first insult to be picked up as a self-identifier and a rallying cry—that's a classic arc for slurs—but it may be the first to have failed so thoroughly as a put-down right from the start. I don't think anyone has ever been hurt by being described as a fierce and tireless fighter for justice.

In truth, so-called social justice warriors are often fighting more for courtesy. The behavior most likely to get you called an SJW is suggesting that it's worthwhile not to cavalierly hurt people's feelings, whether or not you think their feelings are right. Spokespeople for this cause might more accurately, although much less inspirationally, be called social justice butlers: they advocate doing the subtle, sometimes tedious background work of making sure people are comfortable, considered, and not unduly put out. We go not into battle but into buttle.

But the Furies are social justice *warriors*, make no mistake: literal warriors for actual justice. They're the ones who show up when it's too late to keep someone from getting hurt. They don't ask politely for recognition, but demand redress for injury—not just to be made whole but to see the abusers punished. And the idea of this kind of vengeance is so terrifying to a certain kind of man that even its faintest echoes must be mocked into submission. *If we let them demand courtesy, who knows what else they'll ask for? If we let them say "stop hurting us," how long until they say "we seek revenge"?*

People who ask for kindness are called "warriors" to embarrass us, to make us feel like we're overreacting so we're ashamed to ask for more. Those who go to war for justice are called "kindly" to mollify or belittle them. It's a way of pushing us around with words: the euphemisms, the sarcasm, both efforts at control. But it's good to be a warrior, and it's good to be kind. And when the cause is justice, a warrior is the kindest thing you can be.

❧

In the last few years—not by coincidence, the years in which the term "Social Justice Warrior" was created, weaponized, and reclaimed—we've seen a brief, white-hot heyday of female rage. Several books on women's anger came out in the United States in 2018 and 2019: Soraya Chemaly's *Rage Becomes Her*, which touts the personal and social benefits of embracing anger; Brittney Cooper's *Eloquent Rage*, which looks specifically at how black women are reclaiming anger they've long been denied; Clementine Ford's *Fight Like a Girl*, a feminist memoir-manifesto with anger as one of its guiding spirits; Rebecca Traister's *Good and Mad*, which focuses on the way women's anger shaped political action historically and after the 2016 election; and Lilly Dancyger's anthology *Burn It Down: Women Writing About Anger*.

This increased scrutiny of anger—and increased encouragement for women to get in touch with their outrage—coincided, not surprisingly, with a several-year run of high-profile situations in which women were killed, raped, mistreated, harassed, abused, or denied what they deserved. There were the 2014 Isla Vista killings, in which twenty-two-year-old Elliot Rodger killed six people and injured fourteen, explaining his action in a 100,000-word document detailing his sexual frustration and misogynist anger. This was not the first or last mass murder committed by a man aggrieved about women denying him sex, but it was the first to come with a manifesto and to occur at a time when the internet was becoming especially weaponized. (Only a few months later, similarly motivated young men started gang-harassing and threatening women online under the guise of "ethics in games journalism.") There was the 2015 resurgence of the open-secret allegations against Bill Cosby, who would eventually be found guilty of three charges of aggravated assault but not before abusing as many as sixty women over decades, all while maintaining his cultural position as a beloved, trusted father figure. There was the pathetically short sentence given to alleged rapist Brock Turner in early 2016, and the powerful letter from his accuser that elevated the case in the public awareness above all the other pathetically short sentences given to alleged rapists with "bright futures." There was, of course, the 2016 election, in which a flawed but competent woman lost to a heaving garbage pile of a man, despite her being more qualified and more popular. Every aspect of that endless election season, from Trump's menacing loom on the debate stage to the fact that he won despite bragging about sexual assault, was somewhere on the spectrum between a needle under the fingernail and a cleaver to the heart. (This largely held true even if you'd preferred the imperfect woman's first opponent, an imperfect man.) There were the explosive *New York Times* and *New Yorker* articles in October 2017, disclosing how powerful Hollywood producer Harvey Weinstein had been groping and propositioning (and, it came out later, more violently assaulting) women for decades, and threatening or blacklisting those who complained. There was the string of other high-profile allegations: Louis C.K., Roy Moore, Ryan Adams, Chris Hardwick.

But the outrages and abuses weren't new. Men had always been manipulating, abusing, gaslighting, menacing, grabbing pussies, cheating to win, and letting one another off the hook. What was new, what inspired these deep dives into the meaning and mechanism of female anger, was the sense that perhaps this time we'd advanced far enough, fought hard enough, come together enough that something could happen. Maybe, finally, we could ask for justice.

For a brief moment there were millions of Furies: the dozens of abused women who scraped together the courage to share their stories; the hundreds who viewed and contributed to the Shitty Media Men list, feminist writer Moira Donegan's whisper network clearinghouse that collected a lifetime of private warnings about dangerous men in one easily accessible place; the thousands who participated in the hashtags #YesAllWomen, started by a young Muslim woman in response to Isla Vista, and #MeToo, originated by activist Tarana Burke and repopularized in Weinstein's wake. Using the hashtags, women and others shared their experiences of sexual harassment, violence, rape, coercion, abuse, manipulation, and corrosive shame, and then the cleansing anger. It was relentless, a rolling tide of grievance and anguish and, once that spilled over and boiled off, a tectonic ridge of vengeance-hunger, thrusting up through the hot sea of anger like a mountain range where two immovable objects collide. Clearly something was in the air: the desire to see wrongdoers finally named and punished, to drown out the abusers and enablers with the force of our calls for blood.

But at the same time, almost overlapping with this torrential fury, there was an accompanying sense of futility: the realization that the version of justice we were demanding had little in common with any existing mechanisms for punishment or retribution. Many of us knew this already, of course. Black women knew. Tarana Burke had started using the "me too" phrasing all the way back in 2006 to talk about sexual abuse against young women of color, and not much had changed. But black women have never gotten to be the noisy ones. So there was a great swell of noise, amplified by famous and beautiful white women, who have always been allowed to be the loudest as long as they are, paradoxically, mostly quiet. (Though our culture prizes women's silence and docility, it also overvalues white women's pain; the resulting confusion can sometimes be used to great effect in protests.) And then there was a great hush.

I don't mean to say that these burgeoning Furies gave up completely, or even lost hope, although many lost hope (or had been realistic enough to keep their hopes small to begin with). But it became impossible to truly believe in a future where some of these ancient wrongs against us were righted the day Brett Kavanaugh was confirmed to the US Supreme Court—despite being credibly accused of holding a girl down, covering her mouth, and trying to take her clothes off during his high school years. The accuser, Christine Blasey Ford, was sober and consistent in the hearing. As a research psychologist, she effectively served as her own expert witness, explaining the mechanisms of trauma to an audience of powerful men who could not possibly understand and didn't want to. Kavanaugh, for his part, frothed and yelled, his face twisted constantly into a rictus of rage. This anger was his main defense; surely only an honest man could be so affronted. As cultural commentator Lili Loofbourow writes in a *Slate* article: "Ford's anger would have contaminated her motives. Given the reactions to Kavanaugh's tirade, however, it's clear that many still regard *male* anger as not just . . . acceptable but as corroborating: the fact of his inappropriate outburst somehow proves the legitimacy of whatever aroused it. Kavanaugh is angry, so what he's angry about must be true!"

Kavanaugh shouted, and sneered, and lied overtly, and showed himself generally incapable of the comportment and rationality we depend on from the Supreme Court. (Think of the expression "sober as a judge," and then think about Brett Kavanaugh bellowing, "I like beer!") "We expect ordinary people in those circumstances to comport themselves with a modicum of dignity and restraint. For a lifetime appointment, one would think the standards for conduct and temperament would be rather higher," Loofbourow writes. But it worked anyway. He was confirmed—a victory for chaotic, unfocused temper and a blow to Furies everywhere. There could be no clearer emblem of how much systems of order and righteousness had been perverted by the powerful than this: a belligerent, contemptuous, bigoted, almost certainly sexually abusive man being draped in the robes of the law and called "Justice."

The day Christine Blasey Ford calmly unearthed her worst traumas in front of an unmoved judiciary committee rendered every woman I know helpless, useless with rage. (*You are chained in the flow of an active volcano.*) If I'd thought I knew what it was to feel mass anger, the Kavanaugh hearings and their ultimate futility confirmed that I'd only been brushed by its shadow. A friend once said to me that the humidity in summer in DC was less like sweating than like being sweated *on*, and this was how our anger felt in the wake of Kavanaugh: like something that could not come from us, something too big for our bodies, a great beast rubbing up against us and oozing anger onto us from the outside. The possibility of justice, the possibility (never realistic, but once perhaps aspirational) that the law of the land could actually be just, slipped from our sweaty hands.

The Isla Vista shooter became a hero to disaffected young men online, inspiring copycat murders. Bill Cosby was sentenced to three to ten years, but money and power have never protected black men like they do white men. Brock Turner, sentenced to six months, served three. Donald Trump not only grabbed the presidency after bragging on tape about sexual assault but parlayed it into a profitable golf vacation with interludes of cultish praise—despite *more* accusations of rape coming in during his term. Roy Moore, accused of sexually harassing teenage girls, lost his Senate seat but ran again with no shame. Louis C.K., who admitted to masturbating in front of female colleagues against their will, was dropped from a few shows and then returned to comedy less than a year later. Chris Hardwick, accused of emotional and sexual abuse of a girlfriend, hosts two shows on AMC. Brett Kavanaugh is in a position to overturn *Roe v. Wade* in our lifetime. (Harvey Weinstein was sentenced to twenty-three years, a small bright spot.) And the more the indignities have piled up, the harder it is to feel anger through the numbness and the fear. The beast keeps wreathing catlike around us, rubbing its corrosive sweat against our skin, and—like the DC humidity—we've found that it's easier to bear if you just lie still.

But the anger never really goes away, however buried it is under bewilderment and hurt. The Furies, chthonic monsters, are there somewhere, underground.

❧

Justice is not served in *The Eumenides*, either. The trial is a nightmare, really. First, Orestes and Apollo argue that mothers aren't really the parents of their children, just receptacles for a father's seed. This convinces only some people, and the jury votes six to six. Then, Athena, casting the deciding vote, says flat out she only really cares about men, which means she considers Clytemnestra killing Agamemnon a worse offense than Orestes killing Clytemnestra. I like Robert Lowell's translation because it doesn't mince words: "I killed Clytemnestra. Why should I lie?" says Orestes. "The father not the mother is the parent," says Apollo, who adds that the mother is only "a borrower, a nurse." "I owe no loyalty to women. / In all things . . . I am a friend to man," says Athena. "It can't mean much if a woman, who has killed her husband, is killed." Orestes, in other words, is acquitted explicitly on the strength of disdain for women. It doesn't matter if your reasons are good when you control the law.

There are some eerie resonances between the courtroom of *The Eumenides* and our current halls of power and supposed justice. Aeschylus's Apollo might have nodded in approval at the Oklahoma lawmaker who said in February 2017 that pregnant people may "feel like that is their body," but he's more inclined to use the term "host." Women are still punished more for hurting men, even in self-defense, than men are for hurting us. The majority, maybe the vast majority, of women in prison for killing a partner were abused by that person, and yet only a small percentage of domestic violence incidents are ever prosecuted or even reported. This may have looked like justice to Aeschylus, putting words in the mouths of gods and goddesses that tell him he's superior. The gods in *The Eumenides* congratulate themselves often for their enlightened commitment to *real* justice, not the vengeance of the Furies—which is all well and good, in that it elevates reason over violence, but the end result is a murderer goes unpunished (and returns home as a king!) because the judge doesn't think much of women and besides, he's really sorry. (Well, he isn't sorry at all, but he *has* been sprinkled with the blood of a pig, which he says erases his guilt.)

The other end result is that the Furies get a new name. They were historically called the "Kindly Ones" as a dodge, a way to avoid their notice and thus their wrath. But Aeschylus turns it into a condescension, a role bestowed by Athena to dull the sting of justice miscarried. The Furies lose the case, and their punishment, dressed up as a gift, is a new title and concomitant responsibilities: they are now tasked to bestow good fortune on the deserving, not just to punish crimes. (They are also supposed to keep punishing crimes, but now as Athena's right hand and according to her idea of justice, which at this point in the play I find fairly suspect.) "Kindly" in this context is not a euphemism, but a charge: Be less angry, be kinder, be thankful for the chance to grovel. The Furies enter the courtroom as avenging goddesses with their quarry in sight. They leave as declawed do-gooders. Orestes leaves scot-free.

❦

"I did not call myself a feminist until I was nearly 20 years old," Lindy West—who, as a comedian, is worth at least a hundred Louises C.K.—wrote in the *New York Times* post-Weinstein. "My world had taught me that feminists were ugly and ridiculous, and I did not want to be ugly and ridiculous. I wanted to be cool and desired by men, because even as a teenager I knew implicitly that pandering for male approval was a woman's most effective currency. It was my best shot at success, or at least safety, and I wasn't sophisticated enough to see that success and safety, bestowed conditionally, aren't success and safety at all."

As with almost everything, West was several steps ahead of me. I found anger even later, somewhere in my midtwenties, only after I had folded myself softly around so many tiny insults that I was shot through with them. Even at "nearly 20," I never objected to casual misogyny. I laughed it off, let it go, joined in, one-upped. It was a way to cement my position among the carefree perpetrators instead of the angry targets: get offensive, not defensive. If a joke is made at your expense, and it doesn't bother you, was it really at your expense at all? And if you can go one step further—well, who's laughing now?

Mostly, the shit I was shrugging off was directed at someone else. Harassment isn't a compliment, but it does often broadly align with beauty standards because of its trophy element; these men like to demonstrate not only what they're allowed to do, but what they're able to have. And men who believe that their self-appointed power and status entitles them to the bodies or attention of women they find desirable are thrown off by women they don't. Sometimes they befriend us, as a shield: *Look how much I respect women, when I want to.* Often, they're just vicious and insulting, because what they think they deserve instead is our groveling acknowledgment of being beneath their sexual notice.

But of course, I also laughed off or ignored the occasions—less frequent than for women seen as prizes, but still occasional, because none of us escape this—when I did weather undue interest, unwanted touching, men who declined to notice that I was disinterested or uncomfortable or upset or asleep. Anger was, if anything, more unthinkable when I was really the target. To get angry would have been to acknowledge that something was happening; that it was happening on purpose; that it was happening to me. If I wasn't angry, then maybe nothing was wrong.

I didn't think I was doing it for men. I believed it was safer and more comfortable to make yourself soft and porous, to absorb the affronts of the world. I could take a joke, and if that meant taking an insult, well, didn't that mean insults were jokes? But eventually, if you make yourself porous enough, and the deluge never stops, you get waterlogged. I'd absorbed decades' worth of men's contempt.

Anger was a way to boil that out, but first I had to recognize that it was needed. Once you've made these ideas a part of yourself—that male approval will protect you, and that it is won by enduring abuse—even the prima facie absurdity of these inconsistent ideas often isn't enough to stop you from chasing the "chill girl" crown. I had to build anger like a bicep: little by little, complaining all the while.

Fifteen years ago, my mother passed out from altitude sickness, hit her head, and temporarily lost her sense of smell. The problem wasn't damage to her nose, or to her brain. It was to the connections between them: the nerves that transmitted olfactory signals, that turned air molecules into smells and smells into memories. To get it back, she had to retrain those connections, to take a great whiff of what felt like nothing and say to herself: This is gasoline. This is rotten meat. This is a rose.

Learning to be fluent in anger was similar. I knew how to experience the emotion, and I knew (or thought I knew) how to notice when something was unfair, but I'd trained myself out of connecting the two. I had to rebuild the pathway between grief and grievance. That meant learning to recognize the smell of mistreatment, to see it and name it and recognize it as a cause for anger and not for deprecation or self-blame. I listened when other people told me their outrages and took second looks at things I'd laughed away. I took great whiffs of what sometimes felt like nothing: This is misogyny. This is rape culture. This is abuse.

Finding anger was like building a sense, but not the sense of smell—more like a sixth sense. Telepathy, or maybe even telekinesis: a sense of how to move, with my mind, with my words, what had formerly seemed solid. A superpower.

And one of the first things I was able to perceive, with this new sense, was how much it frightened men. Their reactions varied—matching anger, mockery, calls for calm—but the message was clear: Stand down. All the self-protective laughter, all the excuses, all the making myself a concave bowl to hold an insult where it would not hurt: Had those been to protect someone else all along?

〜

One of the origin stories for the Furies is that they were born when Earth, their mother, was fertilized by drops of sky deity Uranus's blood after he was castrated by Cronus, his son (and the father of the Olympian gods). They are, in other words, the literal daughters of emasculation. When a male god is brought low, when his blood is spilled, Furies are born. Their version of justice is not always easy, or clean, and in a moment when the law itself is not just, it may not align with the law. But if we are going to save this doomed world, this is how: by learning to recognize anger and respond angrily where it is called for, whoever it frightens, whoever tries to shut it down.

At a time when anger is the water we swim in, it can feel meaningless, even counterproductive to say this, let alone do it. There are different kinds of anger—never in my life have I felt more aware of the different gradations of its sting. But none of them feel good. Anger, in the body, feels like illness. You want to starve or sweat or vomit it out. You want to place it far away from you, as you would a poison. It is physically uncomfortable; you tense up until your brittle muscles crack like taffy. You wake up stinking of adrenaline from dreams you don't remember. It's not how anybody wants to live.

According to a 2018 study of women's health data, in fact, the constant indignities women are subjected to—being dismissed or ignored or underestimated, getting worse care and less courtesy, being threatened or harassed—have measurable, lasting health effects. The daily frustrations of discrimination add up to one or two points in blood pressure rise over a decade, which sounds small but can increase chances of stroke or heart attack. In other words, poor treatment makes us angry, and anger makes us sick.

This idea, that the anger and frustration born of discrimination is literally bad for your health, isn't new. We've known for a while that worse health outcomes among black people, poor people, and fat people can be at least partially ascribed to racism, classism, and fatphobia. So many people are so justifiably angry, all the time, in ways we're not allowed to express without consequences—and it's slowly killing us.

But what would be worse—to drink from this poison cup and protect it as our right, or to lose the ability to react emotionally when we see a wrong being done? When women are instructed to swallow or put aside our anger, it's not for our health. It's to keep us docile, ashamed to complain or demand or object lest we be seen as monsters. We have been disconnected from our anger, told it's unnatural, unattractive, uncool. We have been taught to repress it to keep men comfortable, to make them less afraid. But our anger comes from injustice, and has justice as its aim. When its presence is the most painful—when we know the law will not protect us, when each indignity is more wounding than the last, when we are almost overwhelmed with it—that is when we need it most.

✑

I somehow managed to not get called for jury duty until I was in my mid-thirties. And I nearly made it through my first time without seeing the inside of a courtroom, though I did get moved from one waiting room to another in a completely different building. But at the drowsy end of a long day of sitting, when I was almost free, they called me in. At the end of the hallway was another waiting area whose glass walls showed a breathtaking view over the bridges of Brooklyn, but we were ushered into a windowless room and told not to speak or read. "I'm just going to tell you," said the judge, "that this is a child sexual abuse case." Then she said twelve names and I was the ninth.

I've heard stories about voir dires in which the assembled potential jurors are asked whether they've ever been assaulted, abused, or groped against their will, and every woman present has to be dismissed. That didn't happen here; we were only asked if we'd been the victim in a court case related to rape or child sexual abuse. Two women left on that one. A few other people were let go on other questions—notably a man who said he "didn't believe in laws," if you ever need to get out of jury duty. And then the rest of us were treated to a chummy monologue from the defense lawyer—he didn't quite pull up a chair and sit down on it backwards, but he might as well have—about how we all know children are untrustworthy and make up stories to get attention or whatever else they want. Didn't we agree?

Some of us, it seemed, did. One older man told us all that he'd been a teacher for thirty years, and in his experience, students will tell any story about why they didn't do their homework. A woman shared similar insights about her children dodging punishment. Neither seemed to notice that even these kids, in their relatively low-stakes situations, were making up stories out of fear. The lawyer nodded encouragingly.

How would I classify the particular sting of this anger? Harsh and dissociating, maybe, like the fluorescent lights of the jury selection room: the vertiginous feeling of looking at your own hands, unfamiliarly grey and veiny in the glare, from somewhere a few inches above your head. Unlike the man who'd been dismissed, I did believe in laws—or the *concept* of laws, the idea that certain actions are corrosive to society or cruel and harmful to other people and should have appropriate, deterrent consequences. Of course the actual design of the law is flawed, and its application even more so, but if anything should be disallowed, it's child abuse. Why was I looking at two unctuous, symmetrical men in suits and a judge with a no-nonsense haircut? Did the moment not call for a swarm of women with snakes in their hair and garments, howling for blood?

I had, of course, confused *law* with *justice*. I have done this often throughout my life, mostly because I'm white and can make that error in blithe ignorance. But I still found myself raising my hand and saying, from somewhere outside myself, "As a matter of principle, in a case of sexual abuse, I start from a place of believing the accuser." Two other women said "Me too."

"All right," said the formidable female judge, who I think was probably a little bit sympathetic. "But this is a jury, and your job would be to maintain neutrality and go on the evidence. Could you do that?" Of *course* I couldn't do that; I was ready to scream "ACCUSATIONS *ARE* EVIDENCE" and kick the smug lawyer in the shin. But I just repeated that as a matter of principle, my baseline is to believe the accuser. (The other two said yes.)

They sent us out for a while to watch the fading daylight gild the Manhattan Bridge. It's truly a beautiful view from the towers of justice. When they called me back in for further questioning, the slick male lawyers seemed less dubious, more condescending: *Surely* I couldn't really understand the implications of what I'd said to them. "Would you be willing to send a man to *jail* on *nothing* but an accusation?" one of them asked. (The prosecutor, weirdly!) "Would you be willing to send him to jail *right now*, just based on knowing he was accused?"

I shrugged. "No, but you're not asking me to do that. You're asking me to sit on a jury for a trial. And if it turned out that nobody had any evidence either way, and the accusation was all I had to go on? Yeah, I'm going to think he's guilty of abuse, not that she's guilty of malicious lying." I am obviously making myself sound more eloquent than I was in the moment—I was shaking—but that's the gist. They did not put me on the jury.

I'm very glad I didn't have to spend a week listening to some pomaded frat boy tell me that a child was inventing trauma for attention. But I'm also very aware that I was deemed a risk for believing in that child's trauma sight unseen—but the schoolteacher and the mother were probably accepted, despite agreeing a priori that she was likely to be lying. Standing up for my principles, which is to say not swallowing my anger or my pride, meant that although I believed the accuser I wasn't there to argue for her. I wasn't able to find any information on the case afterwards, and I'm not sure I really wanted to. If the alleged perpetrator escaped conviction, as 90 percent of reported child sexual abusers do, is that my fault? At least partly, yeah, it is.

We know now, even those of us who were slow to learn, that the law will not bring justice. But what do you do with that knowledge? Do you recuse yourself, and let the jaws of the law grind on? That can't be the answer—but caring too much about justice means that the law will swat you away as an irritant, or even hobble you. The law doesn't want to be challenged; that's why it makes monsters of everyone on the margins.

When the system of law is unjust, committing to justice has to mean abandoning the law entirely, cracking it open like the rotten nutshell it is. Otherwise your commitment is meaningless. I didn't come up with that on my own; Martin Luther King said a version of it, and so did Gandhi. But it is hard, and frightening, and I am weak and privileged and cowardly and certainly no Martin Luther King. Monsters and heroes break the boundaries, but sometimes they get murdered for it, and sometimes they are afraid.

I imagine the Furies filing out at the end of *The Eumenides*, dazed from the undiluted cruelty of the verdict: an official decision, in so many words, that women don't matter as much as men. At first, when the verdict comes down, they threaten to lay waste to Athens, Athena's city. She mollifies them with the promise of power and praise: a new title, new status, a role as her mouthpiece and enforcer instead of her enemy. I wonder, now, if they should have burned the city after all.

DEEP HOUSES

IT'S NOT LIKE YOU COULD ever be fooled into thinking that the House on the Rock is a *normal* house. You approach it via a road lined with giant urns, twice the height of a person, crawling with dark metal dragons. The capacious, wide-windowed visitor's center lobby looks pretty straightforward, but if you need the bathroom after your drive (and you do; Spring Green, Wisconsin, is far from everywhere), you'll find it stuffed with Santa Claus dolls. But it does at least initially appear to be *a house*, in the sense of a place where people could conceivably think to live. The first buildings that visitors traverse, which were also the first ones built, contain the usual house structures: chairs and tables, bookshelves and lamps. It's all a little off—the angles are eldritch, the decor is eclectic, there are more very dark upholstered nooks than you usually want when you're not running an opium den. But it's not a *lot* weirder than Taliesin, the Frank Lloyd Wright building complex seven miles northeast. (The legend, although it is almost certainly not true, is that House on the Rock architect Alex Jordan began his quixotic project as a fuck-you to Wright, who told him he lacked talent.)

But the farther you go into the House, the more its blueprint bulges at the seams. In its depths—because once you leave those first, relatively predictable buildings, it does feel as if you're descending into the hollow earth—are objects of baffling scale, collections of dizzying breadth. There are whole orchestras of self-playing instruments: insert a token into a slot and a room full of uninhabited chairs comes to life with song. There's a 200-foot-tall statue of a toothy sea creature fighting a squid; it fills the center of a massive building the size of an airplane hangar, and visitors circumnavigate it by walking a ramp around the room's perimeter. If you can bear to look at the creature as you circle it—I mostly couldn't, it was too impossibly big and I had to creep up the ramp with my face turned away—you feel like a fly buzzing against its hide. There's an entire old-timey village street inside the House, with shops and a movie theater. There are collections of cars, guns, armor, miniature circuses, all of them at first interesting and then boring and then interesting just for the fact of being so huge and then too huge to even process. At the center of the House is the world's largest indoor carousel: 80 feet in diameter, 20,000 lights, 269 animals, not one of them a horse.

As you move through it, all this garbage, all these wonders, you feel yourself growing and shrinking like Alice. First dwarfed by the whale, then back to human scale on the Streets of Yesterday, then towering over dollhouse after dollhouse after dollhouse. Tiny next to the carousel, then human-size again as you enter a simulated outdoor plaza with a large false tree and a functioning ice cream parlor. (The division between real and fake, too, shuttles back and forth until it blurs into meaninglessness.) And when you get outside and survey the area, you can't see evidence of any structure that actually seems large enough to contain what you just saw.

I am always making my husband go to places like this with me, places I think of as "deep houses." When we traveled to Wisconsin together, we'd been dating for about a year and a half, but—cautious to a fault—he'd only said "I love you" a few months before. This was the next step: a weird building in the Midwest, a three-hour drive from where we'd landed in Chicago. Another year and a half later, I brought him with me to artist collective Meow Wolf's House of Eternal Return, a 20,000-square-foot installation in a former bowling alley outside Santa Fe, New Mexico. This, too, starts as a relatively mundane house: when you enter the exhibition you fetch up on the front lawn of a midsized Victorian, next to the mailbox, amid shrubs and trees. (As with the House on the Rock's ice cream parlor plaza, all of this outdoors is really indoors.) Once you're past the foyer, though, it becomes clear that the house is porous, shot through with portals to surreal worlds. Duck through the fireplace and you'll find yourself face-to-face with a glowing mastodon skeleton. The door under the stairs leads to a tiny jungle of hanging plants. A hole is blown through the wall on the upper floor, leading to a fairy forest full of treehouses and musical fungi. You can even slide through the washing machine into a cramped cavern full of Christmas lights and laundry, trapped in the plastic walls like flies in amber. Eventually you pass full-time into these alternate dimensions, abandoning the house to travel from treehouse to video arcade to alien bazaar to science-fiction travel agency—but every so often you find yourself passing through a door that turns out to be the refrigerator, depositing you back in the house again.

Even if Meow Wolf and the House on the Rock were the only such places we'd gone together (they aren't), that's six thousand round-trip miles we've traveled for deep houses: easily fourteen hours of flights and eight hours of driving. I do it because I love this kind of shit, and thankfully he does too. One of the many ways we align, it turns out, is in our appreciation for buried strangeness. But it started out, a little bit, as a test. If you can't love a house that unexpectedly explodes into strange dimensions, maybe you can't love me.

❧

The creatures that make up Chimera should never be able to even live side by side. She is a three-headed monster, but unlike her sibling Cerberus— the three-headed dog who guards the land of the dead—the heads are nothing alike. She's like a walking game of Rock-Paper-Scissors; eventually the lion must eat the goat, the goat must trample the snake, the snake must sting the lion. And yet none of this happens. She just exists as a single creature composed of her own mortal enemies. Her parts can't quite destroy each other, but they also can't get away.

Like many of the female monsters of antiquity, Chimera earns her greatest fame in her death at the hands of a man. Bellerophon, the only hero who was able to ride the winged horse Pegasus, used his borrowed flight to kill Chimera with her own fiery breath. He tipped his spear with a lump of lead, then aimed it down her throat, where it melted and choked her. Without that meddling kid and his flying horse, though, she could have lived for who knows how long in her state of permanent tension, her irreducible complexity: the domestic head alongside the wild one, the scales with the fur, the horns and claws. A creature who might as easily give poison as milk.

Stories about Chimera—and there aren't many, pretty much just the story of her defeat—don't focus on her complexity as her most monstrous characteristic. This kind of conglomeration was downright commonplace for monsters of Greek antiquity; practically everyone was a snake-woman or a bird-lion or several dogs stuck together. Even Pegasus, the agent of Chimera's downfall, is ultimately just a horse-bird. The trouble with Chimera wasn't that she was a lion-snake-goat. The trouble was that she was a lion-snake-goat who ate people's cattle. But in the centuries since, complexity has been her legacy. Unlike other portmanteau creatures (the horse-eagle hippogriff, the human-lion manticore), Chimera's name has become a synonym for hybridity. The word "chimera" survives to mean anything made of disparate parts: an aggregate creature or machine, an impossible idea, a fantastical beast. Hippogriffs and manticores would be small-c chimeras. A hacked-together computer could be a chimera. So could a turducken.

Scientifically, meanwhile, Chimera has become a metaphor for any plant or animal that contains cells from two genetically distinct creatures. Sometimes that's as mundane as plant grafting, a fairly common gardening technique in which, for instance, a limb from one tree is joined to the trunk of another. A grafted tree or shrub is a kind of genetic chimera. But so is an animal or human being who combined with another zygote in the womb, two fertilized eggs accidentally becoming mixed up in a single creature.

Human chimeras often don't find out until they're grown, if they find out at all. In the course of a routine medical exam, they may discover they have two different blood types. An extra organ might show up on a scan, an organ that had gone unnoticed for decades. Sometimes human chimeras don't find out until they fail parentage tests for their own children, who have the DNA from some lost zygote instead. It's amazing how long irregularities can go unnoticed because they never come to bear.

This type of human chimerism is rare, but another type—microchimerism—may be downright common. A gestating mother donates some cells to her child—not just her genetic material, in the form of a fertilized egg, but her *actual cells*, her own genetic fingerprint. She receives some in return, and those cells stick around forever. Everyone who has gestated, which is some of us, and everyone who has been gestated, which is everyone, has the possibility of containing foreign cells.

And whether they have been pregnant or not, people with two X chromosomes (which includes most women) are also chimeric. Because we only need the genes from one X chromosome, and the majority of women have two, each of our cells chooses one X to express and one to pack away unused. (It's called X-inactivation or lyonization—after geneticist Mary Lyon, not the Chimera's lion head.) We're not, by the strictest definition, genetic chimeras; for the most part, we come from a single fertilized egg, not two. But we are genetic mosaics, chromosomal patchworks in which the gene expression of one cell may not match that of the next.

This is the reason why calico cats are almost always female. Their patchy patterns actually come from random combinations of active and inactive X chromosomes. (Male cats with this coat are always XXY.) For double-X humans, our motley nature is usually less obvious. But we're genetic calicos: every cell hosting a dormant sister, every cell with the echo of what it could have been. Inside each of us, another animal, sleeping.

❧

I started thinking about deep houses and love because a friend asked me to officiate her wedding, which she planned to have at the House on the Rock. It was her second wedding. I'd been a bridesmaid at her first, and then both our marriages had failed, or perhaps we'd just shed them, like old skin. Due to budget and time constraints, she ended up having it instead in her hometown of Baltimore, at the same venue where I'd had my first wedding ten years before. I wrote the ceremony about the House on the Rock anyway, because what else are you supposed to do? I wanted to think about a place I loved, a deep house, instead of thinking about my first wedding. I thought about my first wedding anyway.

Wedding ceremonies often feature a lot of rhetoric about two people becoming one, or sharing a life, or building a life together. Mine had not. Our readings quoted Rilke: "Each partner appoints the other to be the guardian of his solitude." We didn't have a first dance, but it could have been to Dar Williams's "In Love but Not at Peace": "I'll stay in my body and you'll stay in your own, 'cause we know that we're born and we're dying alone." That was my theme song, anyway. I was looking for a ground-floor kind of love, a shallow kind; I was looking for love I could wear as a badge. Being married, knowing someone who was willing to marry me, was the only real proof I could point to that I was an acceptable person—or anyway that someone would accept me, had accepted me. This felt fragile and precious, a veneer of approval I could crack just by moving wrong. Now that someone had pledged to love what he could see, it was vital that he never be allowed to see what he couldn't love.

At home we slept under separate covers, so we didn't have to worry about sharing. I didn't let him open my closet; I would only grudgingly share the trunk of my car, even after his became undriveable. Those private spaces—my closet, my car, the solitary bundle I made of myself in my solitary blanket—weren't concealing any particular secrets; I wasn't cheating, or stealing, or living a double life. I was just a little sadder and angrier than I ever let on—less satisfied than I should have been in our little shallow home in the suburbs, less patient, less at ease, and also more fed up and frustrated at the general state of the world. What was important was not the things I was hiding but the fact of hiding them. Being married meant presenting a simple, appealing, unchallenging face to the world. To be lovable was to be uncomplicated. To be lovable when complicated was to stay unknown.

Besides, in public, or even when it was just the two of us, it was clearly my job to set the emotional tone. If I was visibly pissed off (usually about politics) he would signal for me to calm down; I learned to channel that anger into writing. But if I was visibly glum or discouraged, he would get low too, the weight of my unhappiness thickening the atmosphere in the house until it heavied us both down. Giving in to being sad, having a moment of weakness when I let myself droop, meant having sadness amplified back at me, stronger and more pervasive and now utterly my fault. He would never have yelled—he had an even keel, and wanted me to have one too. Luckily, I'd spent enough time with men who did yell to have plenty of practice in keeping my tone light, no matter what.

It's embarrassing, now, how fully I'd bought into the idea that achieving and sustaining a marriage was my highest goal, even if it meant trying to tourniquet off all my thornier emotions. But it is not, ultimately, all that surprising. Being raised and socialized as a girl means being groomed for marriage. Personally, my mother tried to avoid some of the more obvious pressures—she would leave off the "and then she married a handsome prince" coda from fairy tales, because wasn't it good enough that the dutiful sister is rewarded and the lazy sisters are shamed? But even the idea of the dutiful woman is wrapped up in the idea of the heterosexual wife: the backbone of a family, the solid ground, the handler of everything, the taker of care. It wasn't exactly that I wanted to be "a good wife"—I would have bristled at that, even then. It was that I wanted to be a good person, and when you are raised as a woman, "good wife" is the model you get.

Women are supposed to wife our partners (especially male partners), our bosses, even our male friends—to carry the burden of organizing, planning, remembering the plan, repeating the plan, enacting the plan, thinking ahead, tidying up, keeping track, maintaining friendships, hearing grievances, noticing what needs to be done and doing it, all of it with an even voice and a smile lest our resentment sour the air. With all this resting on us, we can't afford to be erratic. A bad day, an illness, an impulse, and it all falls apart, rattling the delicate Jenga-work we've built of men's feelings and schedules and social lives. We build it on top of ourselves.

☙

A few years after I left my marriage, in the summer of 2015, I wrote an article for the now-shuttered website *The Toast* about women's uncompensated emotional labor. It was published—no lie—on the same day my now-husband and I were visiting the House on the Rock. The idea of emotional labor being designated "women's work" was by no means a new one, nor was the concept of emotional labor generally. In fact, technically I was using the term wrong; academically, emotional labor meant the feelings-related work people were expected to perform as part of a service job. But it seemed to neatly sum up something I'd been thinking about a lot in my postmarriage life: that there are whole categories of difficult work that women are expected to perform without reward or acknowledgment. Not only that, but we're actively shamed for treating these high-effort, high-value services as something that can be bought and sold. We live in a society where you can pay someone money to stand in line for you if you consider your time too valuable, but women are looked on with scorn if they try to pay for cleaning (shouldn't you do that yourself?), sell sex (shouldn't you do that for free?), or—and this was my main focus—ask for recompense or even appreciation for the huge amount of labor we put into managing men's emotional lives. We're not supposed to be given anything in return for this emotional management, and more than that, we're not supposed to *want* anything in return. "Housework is not work. Sex work is not work. Emotional work is not work," I wrote. "Why? Because they don't take effort? No, because women are supposed to provide them uncompensated, out of the goodness of our hearts."

This was a particularly mercenary angle, perhaps because I was a freelance writer living on my own in New York City and acutely aware of putting enormous effort into things I was not being paid for. Within the week, though, a graduate student who went by the username sciatrix posted the piece to the venerable community weblog MetaFilter, and in the resulting discussion—more than two thousand comments!—readers developed an understanding of emotional labor both broader and more nuanced than the one I had offered. They talked about the effort of counseling male friends and partners, and validating the egos of both friends and strangers in order to keep the peace, all of which I'd discussed. To this they added the enormous effort of maintaining social and family ties on behalf of an entire couple, assigning and overseeing household chores even when you're not the one performing them, massaging the egos of men in the workplace, carefully monitoring your tone and word choice when doing all of the above to keep men from bristling and sulking about being managed. And they talked about making yourself and your needs small, turning yourself into a "bonsai human" so you don't overgrow and encroach on someone else. *This discussion changed my life*, people kept saying. *I finally have the words for my feelings now.* I felt the same way.

"I often talk about emotional labor as being the work of caring," wrote MetaFilter commenter Lyn Never. "And it's not just being caring, it's that thing where someone says 'I'll clean if you just tell me what to clean!' because they don't want to do the mental work of figuring it out. Caring about all the moving parts required to feed the occupants at dinnertime, caring about social management. It's a substantial amount of overhead, having to care about everything. It ought to be a shared burden, but half the planet is socialized to trick other people into doing more of the work." User MonkeyToes summed it up: The foundation and fertilizer of unequal emotional labor is "the expectation that women will be naturally, effortlessly skilled at 1) keeping track of what's important to family members, friends of the family, work colleagues; 2) having antennae out for others' invisible and subtle expectations/missives/tone/frequency of contact/mood/needs; 3) noticing entropy and taking note of potential problems; 4) acting as a fixer-facilitator-logistics coordinator; 5) making things comfortable/easy/nonthreatening for others; while 6) doing this on an unpaid basis; 7) doing this on an unnoticed basis; 8) being mocked and/or gaslighted for mentioning the existence of all of this as work, and as exhausting; 9) being called nags and told to lower our standards, because we notice so much; and 10) feeling like we are failing at 'being in charge of everyone's happiness.'" If that was tiring to read, consider how exhausting it is to live.

A 2005 study in the *Journal of Marriage and Family* backs this up: at least among the 335 heterosexually married working parents the researchers talked to, the allocation of "emotion work," like listening to a spouse's problems or doing favors for them, was *more* gendered than housework or childcare, in a way that can't be accounted for by women having more resources or time. This is women's work: listening, caring, noticing, anticipating, keeping track, conveniently all the unquantifiable stuff that can never be accounted for or repaid. Some subsequent articles and comics offered what I think is a better term for this whole constellation, one that doesn't misappropriate a scholarly term: the "mental load."

My ex-husband, like any number of husbands and ex-husbands in the MetaFilter thread, would be able to point to things he routinely did around the house, often without prompting, often things I never did at all: cook, vacuum, make me coffee, mow the lawn. I appreciated these things. I still appreciate them in retrospect. But the inequity isn't limited to a laundry list of domestic tasks. The inequity, in this case, was that he cooked and I did dishes and shopped and cleaned the bathroom, he vacuumed and I spent nearly all of my mental energy on anticipating and planning and social maintenance and noticing what needed doing and worrying about what wasn't done, he mowed the lawn and I restructured my dreams and ambitions to fit my circumstances, he made me coffee and I manhandled all my negative emotions into a small heavy neutron-star lump in my chest so they didn't drag him down. I was a bonsai person, laboring to make myself small.

And how do you prune a multiheaded monster? You amputate.

Chimera's multiplicity outlives her because, unlike the other hybrid monsters of antiquity, she's not simply an agglomeration of fearsome beasts, lion and eagle and serpent and man. That kind of multiplicity makes sense: double a monster's terrible strength by grafting two powerful creatures to-gether. And yet, here's the goat: practical, simple, domestic, content. Wild goats do exist, but the ancient Greeks would have been well acquainted with the goat as reliable farm staple; other goats in mythology include Amalthea, the nanny goat who acted as a literal nanny to the god Zeus when he was an infant, nursing him on her milk and keeping him safe from his vengeful father. The goat doesn't strengthen the lion or the snake—in fact, she's as vulnerable to them as a man might be. What she adds is not new strength, but another kind of fearsomeness: the fear of the irreducible, of the unpredictable. We are suspicious of a creature so vast and multifari-ous that it can even contain its own contradictions.

For women, who are not supposed to be lions or snakes, the domestic goat is not frightening but expected: she carries all the burdens of the home, protects babies and gods and feeds them from her body. She is not only useful but bred to be useful, devoting her attentions and ambitions to the ultimate goal of being functional and tame. It's the other heads that are challenging, unacceptable, dissatisfied; they look out towards the wilderness, while the goat casts her mail-slot eyes over all the tasks that need to be done. They roar and cry and breathe fire. When bonsai women prune ourselves, this is how we do it: by cauterizing our more disagreeable aspects, the heads that don't fit the task. Wouldn't we be better off without the parts of ourselves that don't serve men, that threaten men, that men don't understand? Wouldn't life be simpler as a happy goat? Banish the claws and venom and fire; leave behind something tame that gives you milk.

But Chimera with her other heads cut off isn't a goat. She's just a Chimera who's bleeding.

❧

The Chimera of myth may have her origins in a mountain studded with eternal flames. Several historians (including Pliny the Elder) trace her to a "Mount Chimera" in Lycia, which played host to lions, goats, and snakes—and, like the monster, spouted fire. The geothermally active area of Yanartaş in Turkey fits the bill. Its methane flames spurt forth continuously from the rock, steady enough for hikers to boil tea on. They've been burning for thousands of years.

This practice, of reducing mythology down to real people and places and events, goes by the lovely name of "euhemerism." There's no way to know for sure whether a euhemerizing explanation is the "real" story behind the origins of a myth, but it makes some intuitive sense for Chimera to be something vast and geological—a mountain instead of a monster. Vast things can be various and not tear themselves to pieces; a continent can host many biomes and still be solid ground under your feet.

But a woman is not a continent, and we're not supposed to be so manifold. From the genetic cacophony of our birth, we are expected to forge a simple, predictable self, pushing down any elements that aren't in harmony. There's something seismic about the upheaval that comes when the creatures you've long ignored insist on being born. Sometimes, to fledge yourself, you have to shrug off everything that rests on top of you.

A year before I left my marriage, there was an actual earthquake in my town, the first one most of us on the East Coast had ever experienced. Nobody was seriously hurt; in my house, almost nothing even fell over. But it was existentially unsettling to realize that the earth can shift under you at any time, that what we think of as "earth" is actually just the very outer facade of something turbulent and strange. It may stay quiescent long enough to fool you, but at every moment, the earth has deeper and noisier roots than we know.

We East Coasters had forgotten, in our decades of life on tame ground, that we live on a tenuous shell, a thin coat of paint on top of grinding rock and magma and metal. That's what the earth is, really—not the solid unmoving landscape but the clashing stones and fire. When you recognize that, you can live in harmony with the danger—not perfectly, but better. You can build in a way that shifts with the rolling ground. When you're unprepared, the slightest tremor can ruin you.

❧

I didn't feel, at first, like I was growing away from myself—like I was trying to chop off or curl up any parts that didn't behave. I suppose I just felt like I wasn't growing at all, which at first I just thought meant I'd finished—that I was fully matured as a domesticated goat. But I hadn't finished. I'd just realized, on some level, that growing more would mean changing shape, developing into something I couldn't predict and wasn't supposed to be. And when you truly stop growing—no new skin cells, no new blood—it's called death.

I did feel dead: sleepwalking, dull, cottoned up with disappointments. It wasn't so much that I didn't love my husband; it was that I was starting to think I'd never known what loving someone meant. I'd been so focused on trying to edit myself into something other people could love—I'd just selected someone kind and smart and comfortable who seemed to be fooled. Thinking someone is kind and smart and comfortable is a kind of love. Making yourself palatable for someone else is, I guess, a kind of love too. But not every kind of love is the kind on which you can build a life.

After a few years I wanted my life to be less constrained. I wanted to unfurl everything I'd hidden in order to be presentable, to be marriageable in the first place. It seemed like a foregone conclusion that we would eventually buy a house, have a child; wasn't that what I'd been aiming for, the normal life that would prove I was normal too? But I still felt too underdeveloped, not like a young adult but like a kid: a burgeoning tantrum ready to blow. Under all the dead tissue I'd built up, there was a roiling. I was drum-tight with restless emotion, but still pushing it back down to keep the peace.

I thought a change of scenery might be the answer—leave the dishwater suburbs for somewhere more lively, somewhere that flashed and roared in all the ways I couldn't allow myself. I suggested we look for apartments in Baltimore, less than an hour away, so I could be in a city. He agreed, then decided the commute was too much of a bear. Eventually I said that if we didn't move, I would have to move alone. He kept working in the lab where he got his doctorate, and didn't apply for any other jobs. Another year passed. I kept myself busy with dance classes, art classes. Friends started having children. My journalism job moved to Philadelphia; I could come along, they said, but of course I was stuck. I found a remote job, so I could keep it if we moved. We didn't move. I didn't want to leave, but I couldn't stay. I was crawling out of my skin. Or anyway, something was.

❧

When I left my marriage, it was like being reborn. I don't mean it was like freedom. I mean it was like the violence of birth: pushing out, slicked in blood, from inside a constraining cell. Or maybe it was like limbs, or heads, coming back to life, all needles and pins. Or maybe it was more like the metamorphosis of a caterpillar into a butterfly, where the entire creature dissolves into goo and then is somehow re-formed before it cracks its shell. Almost every part of it blurs in memory, after all: the actual leaving feels dreamlike, the life before like someone else's memories. Who was I when I was goo?

And who was I now? Coming of age as a monster, when in goat years I had already been in my prime, was disconcerting—like going through puberty again, but as a different kind of creature. This second adolescence is something I've seen in almost every woman friend who leaves a stagnant marriage, even those with adolescents of their own. Like a teenager, you are insufferable for a long time, sometimes years: talking about drinking and dating and drugs like you just invented them, trying on new personalities to impress people who are ultimately no one in your life. I even had bizarre hormonal fluctuations, like I was going through actual puberty: hot flashes, night sweats, migraines. And of course, every emotion I'd tamped down came howling out of me, not taking turns, not always at appropriate times. I was raucously, painfully sad, often lying in the dry bathtub and crying for hours at a time. (I did eventually start putting a blanket in the tub first. I could give myself that much care.) I was angry in ways that were mean and petty and unfair, and in ways that were lucid and crystalline and helped me burn off the last of the dead flesh, the last of the people-pleasing false skin I'd been living inside. I got a tattoo of a pangolin: a little armored creature starting to carefully unfurl.

And then, after the night sweats, after the period of change, my adolescent claws started to come in. My monster self grew less coltish, stronger: wings unfurling, horns sharp. I stopped vomiting emotions. I held them now like a coal in the chest waiting to be unleashed in a breath of fire. When you're whole, there becomes, all of a sudden, such a thing as balance.

I had not fully finished monster puberty when I met my now-husband, but I was on my way. Being in a city, as it turned out, did help. All my unmanageable emotions simply blended into the chaotic background, the way anxiety dissolves under loud enough percussion. I had my own tiny apartment, at ruinous expense, because I was in no shape to live with someone else. When I'd moved in, I'd slept on a pile of clothes and used a folding chair as a kitchen table, but now I had a bed and a sofa and a coffee table made out of a giant clock someone had put out on the curb. I had found some friends who were the right amount of adventurous, and I was rediscovering what kind of adventures I liked, now that I could have adventures again. (One of my favorites was a cocktail party in a cemetery, winding our way down dim paths lined with candles and into a catacomb filled with cocktails and music: an early deep house.) I was starting to write things I was proud of, at least for a moment, once in a while. And so, when I encountered this other DC escapee who riffed off all my jokes and knew all my words and had things in common with me I'd never thought to ask for, I could tell not only how he would fit into my life, but that it was *my* life he was fitting into, actually mine.

Six months or so after we got together, my sister got married. The date she had chosen was my former anniversary. She'd asked me if it would be weird, and I had said "I guess not"—by instinct, mostly, because I was still so accustomed to ignoring any emotions that might deform the space around me, anything that might bring down the room. My boyfriend knew better. He showed up with a box of candy and another box of fancy candy-colored cigarettes. We didn't even smoke, not really, but he knew what the situation would call for, even when I didn't: a festive atmosphere, a bit of sweetness, a chance to step outside. He was ready to let me admit when something felt bad—or not admit it, and just take the comfort offered.

In the end, it was fine. The wedding was beautiful. Nobody mentioned the date to me. My boyfriend smiled gamely at a lot of family members who he couldn't hear and whose names he didn't yet know. I nailed my speech, which was about how my sister has always had a clear and perfect vision of how her life will go, how she has never compromised her ambitions. I smoked exactly one bright green cigarette: just a wisp of sadness subsumed in someone else's good time, just a hint of fire on my breath.

❦

It would have been easier, in some ways, if my ex-husband was the monster, instead of me. If he'd been cruel, if he'd betrayed me, it would have hurt more but made a cleaner story, maybe even one that let me off the hook. But he wasn't the one who asked me to tuck away my teeth and claws. I did that on my own. I thought it was the price you paid for love. He didn't notice I was hiding them—but why would he? I didn't even notice, not really. I just wanted to stay happy enough for our home to be happy, helpful enough for our home to be good. For women who have tried to bow to the demands of simple domesticity, our own selves can often sneak up on us. What looks like a single creature is two, or more. What looks like a home is a cavern of visions. What looks like a solid mountain is pitted with flame.

When you've spent all your life smothering your contradictions, their eruption can undo you. But it's not being a chimera that confounds you. Most of us are born that way. It's the years spent trying to simplify yourself, to present a domesticated and reliable facade, to take responsibility for carrying calm and contentment into the home and never letting it drop. If you'd always been allowed to be angry, sad, strange, contradictory—lion and goat and snake, venom and milk and fire—imagine how strong you'd be.

This is why deep houses are a test for me: because they make you reckon with complexity. You may step at first into a mundane parlor, a scene of pure domestic pragmatism: the friendly face of an easy, livable home. But it's a thin veneer, cracking almost from the start. There's a mastodon behind the fireplace, a crystal cave in the closet, a science fiction travel agency inside the fridge. There are strange, obsessive accumulations of ersatz junk. Everything is vertiginously bigger or smaller than it ought to be; everything feels disorienting or dazzling or downright dangerous. When you look at it from the outside, there's no way there's room for all of this, but here it is.

That's what it means, I think, to love someone wholly: to venture beyond the living room, into the depths. It may seem like a kindness to confine them to the upper floors, where things are predictable, usable: tables, chairs. But shutting the portals also means locking them out of the psychedelic treehouses, the hanging gardens, the empty rooms that suddenly burst into music. The collections of days and moments and conversations laid out like rows upon rows of miniature circuses, all the same and yet somehow always surprising. The vast madly spinning thing at the heart, adorned with twenty thousand lights.

I have made my husband travel six thousand miles with me, and more, to crack the skin of domesticity and dig into the strange labyrinths underneath—to make sure he can handle it, and also, because I know he can. When I find more deep houses, and I will, we'll visit them together; I don't need, or want, to go alone. The wilder heart will always exist, but sometimes it doesn't say "go." Sometimes it says "I'm going. You come too."

SHARK, SNAKE, SWARM

N 2008, WHEN MY mother's mother was still alive and not yet losing her memory, my cousin Andrew interviewed her in a StoryCorps booth in Foley Square in Lower Manhattan. She was eighty-four years old and in relatively good health. A year before, she had moved from the Queens rowhouse where she'd been rattling around for a decade since my grandpa died, and now she was living in a studio apartment on the Upper West Side. She had a boyfriend in her building, was in a book club, went to see films of opera productions around the corner at Symphony Space. "I love getting older," she told Andrew in the interview. "I didn't think I would."

At the beginning of the tape, she expressed some concern about being asked personal questions: "There are some things grandsons don't need to know." Andrew reassured her that he didn't mean *that* kind of personal; he just wanted to talk about her, not other people in the family. Not her parents or children—just her.

"May I just interject one thing?" she said, and then, as she always did, went right ahead. "One day I was standing in front of my living room. I was taking care of my nephew, because his mother, who is my sister, had to go to work. I was also concerned about my parents. I had two children, a husband, two sisters, and I stood in the middle of the floor and said, 'I don't want to be anybody's mother, sister, cousin, daughter, wife. I want to be me.'" This was delivered with a flourish—picture the panache of Frank Sinatra drawing out "myyyyy wayyyyy," but aggressively unmusical.

("What will you give me if I don't sing?" she would say when she called on my birthday.)

Andrew, I assume, had heard this story before. I had heard it before. It was always softened, afterwards, with the acknowledgment that she *couldn't* possibly isolate herself from her relationships: "And then after I said it, I said, well, how would I define me? That's who 'me' is." But to me, that part never rang true—not as true as "I don't want to be somebody's mother," anyway. It was a moral tacked on to make all of us feel better, to reassure us and herself that she had no regrets. She couldn't fully commit to it, though. When my cousin paraphrased—women of your generation, he said, and you particularly, really do define yourself by roles like "mother" and "wife"—she corrected him. "But I resented it," she said, "because I do not truly define myself by that, but these are responsibilities thrust upon me, which I could not deny. How could I?"

Did you always know, Andrew asked, that you were going to be a mother? She cut in: "No. No, I was not going to do any of that. But it happened."

At one point, she claims that she never thinks about what her life would have been like if she hadn't gotten married. But after just a little pushing, it turns out she knows exactly what she would have done: "I would have been a bum. I would have traveled all over the world, I would have had no responsibilities, I would have taken whatever job would give me the ability to travel, because I always was hungry for travel. And I would have been maybe lonely, but I wouldn't have had worries."

Throughout the interview, you can hear my cousin trying to prod her into talking about how proud she is of her family. This is an image of my grandmother that much of my family has always clung to, the kvelling matriarch, even as she told us over and over that it wasn't the entire story. I don't mean to imply he didn't appreciate what she was saying about resenting the loss of independence; he did, I think, but he was also only twenty-three. At that age, you don't want to hear your grandmother, the linchpin of the family, say that her relationships have mainly brought her grief. "A lot of these questions on this list that I printed out are like, what are you proudest of, what matters to you the most, and I don't know but

I think the family would be a big part of that for you," he prompts at one point. She considers this. "Yeah," she says doubtfully, "because it was thrust upon me. And here it is."

This interview is hard for me to listen to, but not because part of her wishes I'd never been born. What is difficult is, first and foremost, that she is dead, which was the last thing she wanted. I mean, it's the last thing anyone wants (and, of course, the last thing they get), but somehow she wanted it *less*. A staunch lifelong nonbeliever—Andrew once trolled her with an elaborate April Fool's prank involving a letter saying she'd been chosen for a church Adopt-an-Atheist program—she became, as she aged, increasingly fixated on how impossible it is for those without religion to make peace with death. "I'll be ready to die once I've found God," she always said, with the implied wink: *I'll live forever.*

It worked for a long time—she lived to ninety-two. But ultimately, death doesn't wait for you to be ready, no matter how good of a joke it is. We scattered some of her ashes, surreptitiously, on a rose bush in the median of Broadway, across from Symphony Space. I took home some of the rest; they're above my TV, in a little box with an infinity symbol on it, like the one on her gravestone. This is not a reference to some sort of supposed infinitude of the soul, which she would have scoffed at; it's just an acknowledgment of one of her most annoying and endearing habits, which was demanding that you explain the concept of infinity and then looking dubious and declaring she would never understand. Her other favorite bit was "With the brain God gave you, how could you believe in him?"

My grief trips me up when I listen to the interview. Her grief—mourning the life she didn't get to have—does not. Or rather, I don't take it personally; it doesn't make me feel like she loved us any less. Quite the opposite really. My grandmother was one of the most generous people I've ever known, always opening her home to family and strangers alike. (Half of my mom's cousins lived in her basement at some point. So did a girl named Karen, who had been a student aide at Grammy's school secretary job. When her mom kicked her out, Karen moved into the basement and stayed through college. As a kid, I just assumed she was some kind of cousin too.) In true Jewish grandma fashion, she took on your troubles as if they were her own, whether or not she understood them, whether or not you wanted her to. But she didn't experience this as generosity, because she didn't consider there to be any other alternative. You couldn't deny someone in need what it was in your power to give. You couldn't not take care of children, your own or other people's. You couldn't leave the gift ungiven, the loan unlent, the teenager without a home. There was something truly Talmudic about it, not only the righteousness but the sense of being *afflicted* with righteousness, as Jews are always afflicted by something or other. She got it from her own very Jewish mother, maybe, or from her socialist father: a sense that if you have, you owe. Anyway, it was a duty, not a choice. She wasn't especially happy about it, but she had to. She brushed off praise: "What else was I supposed to do?"

That's how you knew her love was truly unconditional: if she *could* have loved you less, if she could have cared less, if she could have given less, she certainly would have. The fact that she didn't was proof that she couldn't possibly. Most people who tout unconditional love still think they have some kind of option. She knew she didn't. My grandmother didn't love anyone she didn't feel she had to, but her love, once given, was an obligation to both of you: it could not be turned off or turned aside.

So I know that, as dubious as she sounds on the tape, my cousin was right. She did define herself by her role in the family, and it was a lot of what mattered to her the most. And her family was also, at the same time, a yoke and an anchor. She *could* imagine life without them, and always had—but no matter how much she wished to be footloose and worry-free, she couldn't regret them, or imagine devoting them anything less than her life. What else was she supposed to do? She was someone's sister, daughter, cousin; she became someone's mother and wife, and someone's aunt and great-aunt and grandma and great-grandma. It was thrust upon her, and here it was.

In fact, I may be the only person still wishing she'd gotten a chance to be a bum. I don't think she mourned her lost life, exactly, but I do mourn it. What breaks my heart when I listen to the interview is realizing that the world has lost her twice, both the matriarch she was and the carefree traveler she didn't get to be. Maybe that's why we understood each other, the thing we shared: recognizing that there is something to be lost in having a family legacy. That if you don't kill the possibility of children, they will kill some part of you.

❧

Most cultures have a female monster who preys on pregnant women, fetuses, newborns, and children. It's a near-universal nightmare: the creature who rips babies from the womb or steals them from the cradle. Her name is Abyzou, Penanggalan, Lamashtu, La Llorona. Her purpose is sometimes to scare children into compliance, but it's often to scare women into compliance as well. Only monsters stand in the way of the natural order: women as incubators, as conduits for birth.

In ancient Greece, the baby stealer's name was Lamia. The myths agree on her name, and her role as a murderer of children, and that's about it. Her backstory and her appearance vary almost psychedelically from story to story. In some, she is a sea monster; her name is the ancient Greek for a rogue shark. In others, she is half-woman, half-snake—or, as in Keats's poem "Lamia," a multicolored snake with a woman's mouth. In some, she is even plural: the Lamiae, a swarm of vampiric demons. She also appears in a seventeenth-century bestiary with a woman's face and breasts, a four-legged body, front paws, back hooves, scales, and a penis and testicles. Unlike so many of her sister monsters—snake-haired Medusa, lion-bodied Sphinx—the important feature of Lamia is not what she looks like, but what she does. The fear of the monstrous mother can have many faces, many forms.

In fact, that multiplicity is part of the fear. There are so many ways to be a mother wrong, so many ways to ruin a child. There's not being able to get pregnant. There's choosing to never get pregnant. Getting pregnant, but not giving birth. Giving birth, but not raising the child. Raising a child, but doing it with the wrong person. Raising a child alone. Raising a child you did not give birth to. Raising a child, but not wanting it enough. Wanting it too much. Expecting too much. Living through your child. Bragging about your child. Regretting your child. Envying your child. Giving your child too little. Giving your child too much.

None of these are fundamentally wrong, of course, but every one means you may be viewed as a threat, a perversion of the natural order. Not the real natural order—there have always been women who are infertile, women who don't have uteruses, women who don't have children or don't want them or raise them in a way that's frowned upon—but the order that is imposed by those who grant themselves the right to speak for nature. To deviate in any way from the prescribed motherhood narrative is to be made a monster, a destroyer of children, whether you do so by trying too hard or not hard enough, providing too much or too little. The acceptable narrative is this: procreate, nurture, and disappear.

∾

In one of my most cherished photos of my grandmother, we are squinting into the sunlight, our hair the exact same color: mine still blonde, hers not yet white, or anyway she hasn't admitted it. I am wearing a truly dreadful color-blocked anorak and white leggings that are baggy at the knees, and holding a sign that says "Pass the Freedom of Choice Act Now." She has one tucked under her arm that says "I Am the Face of Pro-Choice America." It is 1992, and Planned Parenthood gave us those signs, and we are in downtown DC with my sister and some of my neighbors (also in the photo) and my mother and 500,000 other people (not pictured) at the March for Women's Lives. Neither of us looks especially good in this photo, her because the sun is so bright and me because I'm twelve. But I love it because it shows a bond deeper than family: the shared conviction that reproductive freedom is a moral good.

At this march, or maybe another one—there was another March for Women's Lives twelve years later, and then the Women's March another twelve years after that, my life segmented into even dozens by the same weary protest—my mother grew frustrated with the chants of "What do we want? Choice! When do we want it? Now!" "We *have* it now," she complained. (We did have it, although many people who need abortions can't access them, no matter how legal they are.) "We want to *keep* it." Perhaps unsurprisingly, her attempt at a "What do we want? Choice! When do we want it? Later!" chant did not catch on. But I still think about it all the time, and not only at marches. It's good to have a choice now. It's better to have a choice perpetually.

Pregnant people who don't want to be pregnant anymore will always have some choice, though if the right wing gets its way the choice will no longer be safe. Banning abortion has never stopped abortion and never will; it can only increase deaths, which is what it's meant to do. But each of us, individually, will eventually run out of time to choose. There's a point at which you can't conceive a child, if you have a uterus and eggs; there's another, later point at which it becomes physically difficult or impossible to adopt. I know this, and yet. I want to have my choice and keep it too.

❧

About one in four US women has had an abortion by age forty-five. (The available statistics are framed as being about women, but the number is probably about the same across all people with uteruses regardless of gender.) This statistic is an average over the whole population—specifics vary according to factors like class and race, since for instance it's much easier to get an abortion if you have disposable income and transportation. But just to give you a sense of the numbers, that's approximately, say, one abortion per brunch. Eight in a workout class, thirty in Congress, fifty at a showing of *Magic Mike XXL*. At one night of the Bikini Kill reunion tour: 1,250 abortions, at least.

Most of these are not discussed, because who wants to be a monster? Abortion may be as old as civilization, if not older, but so are the stories about Lamia and others like her: the baby-eaters, unnatural. But the truth is, those monsters are everywhere. Abortions are unnatural the way soap is unnatural: man-made from organic materials, and ubiquitous, and good.

In 2015, in the midst of yet another right-wing push to strip funding from Planned Parenthood, activist Amelia Bonow posted on Facebook about getting an abortion at a Seattle Planned Parenthood office the previous year. "I am telling you this today because the narrative of those working to defund Planned Parenthood relies on the assumption that abortion is still something to be whispered about," she wrote. She ended her post with the hashtag #ShoutYourAbortion—as in, shout, don't whisper.

Bonow and writer Lindy West, who cocreated and helped to publicize #ShoutYourAbortion, both said in different publications that they'd realized they didn't regularly talk about terminating their pregnancies, despite being grateful and unashamed, despite being outspoken feminists in other ways. That's how strong the pressure is to keep your voice low. Once West and Bonow gave people permission to shout, though, the shouting was thunderous: tens of thousands of women and others sharing stories about a choice that was hard or easy, scary or reassuring, deeply controversial and deeply normal. A horde of little monsters. Lamia's brood.

Previous attacks on Planned Parenthood had been met with the insistence that the bulk of the organization's services are crucial medical care—Pap smears, contraception, STD tests, transition hormones, prenatal checkups—provided to low-income or uninsured patients. It's lifesaving stuff, and anyone who truly cares about women's health or human life in general should sing its praises. All of this is true, but Planned Parenthood also provides abortions, and they're lifesaving too. The commonly cited figure is that only 3 percent of Planned Parenthood's services are abortion-related, but health centers provide more than ten million services per year to millions of patients (many of whom get multiple services). If the 3 percent number is true, that's still well over 300,000 abortions annually. And yet we are supposed to believe that every single one of these people is a monster for not wanting to be pregnant, or simply for not wanting to be pregnant right now. (Per the nonpartisan Guttmacher Institute, something like 60 percent of people who get abortions are already mothers; others will become mothers later on.)

Opponents of abortion will tell you they believe it's infanticide, but this is for the most part a sham. They're not invested in children, or even in mothers—the same people generally oppose paid maternity leave, subsidized child care, universal health care, social support programs benefiting mothers with kids, and sometimes public schools. They're not invested in reducing abortion—the same people oppose comprehensive sex education and accessible contraception. They're not even invested in reducing deliberate death. Anyone who still believes the "pro-life" spin after months of watching the GOP downplay coronavirus, kneecap efforts to supply hospitals or limit spread, and call for the sacrifice of tens of thousands on the altar of the economy is using a twisted definition of "life." What they are invested in is *birth*: the conversion of a woman into a mother, after which she and her baby can be left to struggle. There are any number of reasons for this, but they all have to do with locking women down. There are so many things you can't do with a child to take care of. There are so many things you won't do if you're afraid of getting pregnant. Women are not supposed to do any of those things.

And so we are all monsters: the one in four who's had an abortion, and those of us who haven't but haven't needed one either. Anyone not involved in the woman-to-mother assembly line. The vampiric swarm of lamiae.

❧

Before Lamia killed children, her children were killed. The root of her violence, like the root of so much violence, is grief. The god Zeus tended to impregnate any woman he fancied, and he fancied her. The stories don't specify how she felt about the arrangement, but these kinds of stories rarely dwell on how any woman feels. Anyway, she got pregnant, and anyway, she had his children. When his wife, Hera, got wind of yet another clutch of bastards, she destroyed them. Lamia turned her grief first inward—in some stories, she plucked out her own eyes—and then outward, murdering other children out of envy and revenge. She doesn't kill children to keep them away from her. She kills them because she wants her children back.

Lamia the snake gets her loops around children and pulls. She holds too tight; she won't let go, even when she should. Wanting children too much—grieving infertility or loss, coveting others' children or having ambitions for your own—is no less a violation than not wanting them at all. Women are seen as unnatural when they don't want to have children, but having them doesn't free you from suspicion, because you could have them for the wrong reasons: living through them, trying to fix your own mistakes, having something to prove. Being jealous of other, better women's other, better children—or wanting other women to be jealous of you. Hungering for unconditional love, and not knowing another way to get it.

Having children seems to turn you (in the eyes of society) from A Woman into A Mother, as if you've passed from pupa to adult by fulfilling your function. But this new creature, A Mother, is subject to the same constraints: Don't want too much, don't aspire too far, don't think too highly of yourself. If anything, it's worse to have ambition or envy or hysteria on behalf of your child. You're supposed to fade into the background, not stay front and center with your large and noisy feelings about what your child is supposed to achieve, or what she deserves, or what's wrong with her. In the nineteenth century, mothers used to cover themselves with a cloth to hold their babies for photographs, so they could keep the children calm invisibly. The result is eerie, an infant perched on a draped black backdrop or a lumpy brocade chair that is just a *little* too human-shaped for comfort. These "ghost mother portraits," I've often thought, represent the pinnacle of expectation for mothers. The ideal relation to childbearing is at worst resignation, at best dutifulness: no personal axe to grind.

It is no better to smother a child than it is to neglect them. It is no better to overfeed than it is to malnourish. It is no better to have too many than too few, to want them too much than to want them too little. This is Lamia's lesson: that a mother, in any form—shark or snake or swarm—is bad for a child. The only proper thing for a mother to do is dissolve.

❧

There are people who are sure they want children. At our grandmother's funeral, I asked my sister, whose daughter was then a year and nine months old, whether she planned to have another. She told me "I've always pictured myself with two." This was absolutely incomprehensible to me—pictured yourself? With children? Pictured yourself in the future at all?—but as with most of my sister's predictions about her life, she knew it with certainty and made it come true. There are also, of course, people who are sure they don't want children, and though they're fighting uphill against expectations, they at least have the benefit of clarity. But what if you're not sure, and worse, what if you suspect you'd do a bad job? That's the kind of fear that stalks the water, no matter what you do: When will I regret this? When and how will I fuck it up? No matter which choice you make, it's potentially the biggest mistake of your life: the slow-roll pervasive sadness of regretting the children you didn't have, or worse, the acute toxicity of regretting the ones you do. Worst of all, the late-stage regret when you realize that you did so badly that you shouldn't have started at all.

What's frightening about sea monsters, like Lamia in her shark form, is both that they are huge and that they are hidden. The scariest part of *Jaws* isn't the blood and teeth; it's the waiting, the low slow stalking music before the attack. The fear comes, at least in part, from watching children run heedless into the water, not knowing what lurks there.

Women are seen as monsters when they don't give a child the chance at life, but also when they do. Because once you do allow an egg to be fertilized and develop into a baby, or once you do go through the process of bringing a child into your home, or once you in any way put yourself in the role of "mother," you take on the outsized ability to ruin someone else for life. Anything can do it, or at least that's what we're led to believe. Lamia seems to have eaten them, mostly, but it's sufficient to be too permissive, or too strict, or too capricious.

I'd probably be all three. I like children, but I also keep strange hours, am highly sensitive to shrill or harsh sounds, hate having to do more work than I think is fair, and very often want to be left alone. I work hard to be a compassionate person, but I'm less sympathetic to people's needs the noisier they are. I'm a prime candidate for ruining a child by being too neglectful or too grudging—not to mention passing on my own anxiety and often gloomy outlook. What happens if I resent them? There's no way they wouldn't know. What happens if I stand in the living room saying "I don't want this, I want to be me," and there's no mollifying follow-up, just the truth we both have to live with: I gave up everything for them and wish I could take it back? I've seen that happen. It wrecks people, mothers and children alike.

For me, this is the most frightening kind of mother-monster who might lurk in my future. I've never had an abortion, but that's pure chance of not needing one; I've never been afraid to, or even unwilling. I do worry about putting too much burden on any future child, but it's not my greatest fear. My greatest fear is the shark under the surface: the huge mass of resentment, scything through the water when you least expect it to swallow a child whole. To be natural, we are told, women must have babies. But how natural is it to let a child be born just to be destroyed?

&

It is the prerogative, perhaps even the chore, of grandmothers to nag you about getting married and having babies. Mine always declined. It was perfectly fine with her if I wanted to live in sin, not that she ever would have called it that, not that she believed in sin. She always wanted to know if someone's partner was "special," but not so she could plot your wedding—just so she knew whether it was time to turn on the bright spotlight of her love, or whether she could stay blessedly indifferent.

After I did get married, the first time, she broached the subject of children only once. "I don't know," I said, "but I'm really enjoying not having them right now." She nodded. "All I would ask," she said, "is that if you don't have children, don't have them because you *chose* not to have them. Don't let time make up your mind for you."

I am on the verge of disappointing her, though she's not around to know it. In terms of sheer age, I'm well past peak fertility, and in terms of my personal reproductive system, I might never have been fertile at all. Time (and endometriosis) may have made my mind up, at least as far as biological children go. And yet I have never been able to fully choose. For a while, I was sure I would have children, but that's not the same as saying I wanted them; what I wanted was to do what would make me feel normal, and acceptable, and loved. Then I was sure I wouldn't, but that was mostly practical—first because I couldn't imagine having children when I was so unhappy, and then because I was divorced and hurtling towards my midthirties. Neither idea was especially inspiring to me; neither was especially distressing. I feel a twinge at the idea of never seeing a child graduate from college, as bourgeois of a dream as that may be. Higher education has kind of lost its cachet now that it's mostly a debt factory that churns out workers, but another one of my grandma's favorite stories involved cradling my infant mother and whispering *"You* are going to *college."* The dream in that story dies hard. Anyway, you can substitute any accomplishment here, really; the thing I'm missing out on is being proud. Is that twinge stronger or weaker, though, than the twinge I feel at the idea of waking up at 4 a.m. every day to feed something out of my body? Or the thought of all the different types of freedom and ease—money, time, space, quiet—that collapse as soon as a baby comes on the scene? Or the stark horror of thinking I might screw them up, and also knowing that I will? The absolute depths of worry I'd be privy to, worry like I've never known, even though I am a very worried person already. The inevitable moment, in a future where I had children, where I would stand in front of my living room and say "I don't want to be somebody's mother, I want to be me." The possibility that I might not go on to think "but this is who 'me' is."

This isn't even getting into the general state of the world, which is both the most and least important consideration. The truth is that, as much as we are all thundering towards oblivion together, in many ways I am buffered from the worst. My child would be too, at least a biological child: we'd all be white and financially solvent and not look especially Jewish, although we'd also be weaklings who don't own a car or a gun (I'm not sure what kind of apocalyptic scenario we're looking at here, but it's best to fret about them all). I'd be bringing a child into a bad world, and from a climate burden perspective I would make the world worse by doing so, but both of us would be insulated from the immediate consequences of that decision. This isn't a reason to do it, but it's true. On the other hand, though, right now it's a comfort to me that at least when the end comes, my husband and I will be able to lie down and quietly die together—or rather, my biggest fear is that we won't, that we'll be separated or worse. When I said I was a worried person, this is what I meant—that I go through our cabinets wondering how long we'll be able to survive on dry noodles; that I fret about how accessible our windows are from the street, not because of crime but because of a post-apocalypse Purge. (All of this was in some way put to the test during the long nightmare of coronavirus, though food shortages and roving bandits weren't as much of a problem as I'd imagined. It turns out I was right in most respects. No amount of dry noodles is enough to feel safe, but it's better to be together.) That anxiety is not only compounded by the addition of a child; it's increased exponentially, because not only do I have yet another life to worry about, a life I will by all accounts be even more disastrously concerned about than I am about my husband or dog, but I am virtually guaranteed that even if the end doesn't come in my lifetime, it will in theirs.

None of these thoughts are especially unique, and all of them add up to *I don't know*. I have not known for many years, through nearly the entire run of my hypothetical fertility, and I am no closer to knowing. Maybe knowing isn't as important as just deciding. But part of me is waiting to say "What else was I supposed to do?"

～

In some versions of the story, Zeus gives Lamia the power to take out her eyes and put them back in at will. The reasons for this are murky. It may be because as a human—after her children were killed, but before she became a shark or snake or swarm—she plucked out her eyes in grief. It may be that she was cursed to be unable to escape the image of her dead children, and Zeus offered her the option to remove her sight as an act of mercy. In some stories, this curious gift comes even before the loss of her babies, and stems from Zeus's fear of his wife: Lamia's removable eyes let her stand guard even as she sleeps.

The story changes form like Lamia does, first one thing and then another. The monster of failed motherhood is a shapeshifter; she will never hold still. She will change to reflect your worst fears, or someone else's: the mother trying too hard, the mother with regrets, all the potential mothers saying "no" or "not now." Being seen as a woman, being understood as a potential mother, means flickering between these monstrous forms until you choose one, or it chooses you.

Ambivalence is comfortable, a neutral-buoyancy tank: neither too much mother nor too little, but a permanent pause. Eventually you run out the clock, and time, as my grandmother said, makes your mind up for you. But for a brief period, you float weightless, pulled on every side by forces so contradictory that they leave you suspended in space. It's no surprise I don't want to drop. It's no surprise I don't want to choose the shape of the nightmare I'll become.

Faced with all these worries, all these monsters you could be, Lamia has a single boon: the gift of not looking. This is all we are given—the freedom not to know which way we'll fail. There is no guaranteed choice, no guarantee even that a choice will be available. There is the expected thing, which is impossible: become a mother at the cost of being a person. Then there's a panoply of wrong decisions, bright and variegated as Keats's depiction of Lamia's multihued scales: "vermilion-spotted, golden, green, and blue; / Striped like a zebra, freckled like a pard, / Eyed like a peacock, and all crimson barr'd." Nonmotherhood, delayed motherhood, early motherhood, envious motherhood, long-desired motherhood, regretted motherhood, outsourced motherhood, medically disastrous motherhood, psychologically disastrous motherhood, motherhood disasters of every color and stripe. All of them ruin someone or something. All of them cut off some version of the future, forever. All of them are potentially the worst mistake you'll ever make. None of them are inevitable—but you won't know until it's too late.

❧

In May 2019, after several states passed near-total abortion bans that flew in the faces of both law and medical science, I went to a Planned Parenthood rally in Foley Square. I told people I was planning to spend the evening "shouting about abortion," but in truth, I didn't shout much. I rarely want to shout these days—or rather, I always want to shout, and the very wanting saps my energy to the point where I can't always make my lungs obey. A week earlier, the online humor magazine *Reductress* had published an article about abortion rights headlined "Aww! These Three Generations of Women Have All Been to the Same Fucking Protest." This was funny but also an understatement. I'd already been to reproductive rights protests with three generations of my family, and I was almost forty. We could easily have been on generation four.

It was a beautiful day, balmy and bright. Ringed with tall buildings, Foley Square was already cupping early twilight in its palm, but home-made signs turned their faces to the sun like hopeful plants: *Abortion Is a Human Right, My Body My Choice, Never Again.* To my left, early-evening light gilded the motto inscribed on the front of the New York County Courthouse. The only word I could read from where I stood was "justice."

My friend and I hung just inside the crowd, straining to hear the speakers but also intermittently dropping into conversation. We clapped at applause lines, even if we weren't sure what they'd said. We listened with mild schadenfreude for that last "No hate, no fear!" that always rings feebly out after the chant has braked, like a kid going over the handlebars of a bike. Doing more felt perilous, like we might overexert our already aching hearts. At one point, an older woman came winding through the crowd, shouting "Over ninety coming through!" In her wake was an even more elderly lady with a floppy pink sunhat and a rolling walker, bowed by age and a heavy plating of pro-choice buttons. She didn't look anything like my late grandmother, apart from being over ninety, but she looked exactly like her too.

The StoryCorps booth where Grammy had told Andrew about resenting her responsibilities was behind us, a little outside the crowd. As the rally died down, I picked my way over to it, through the dispersing bodies, over chalkings that read "Fuck your ban" and "We won't go back." It's a large glass box, about the size of a shipping container, with "Listen. Honor. Share." inscribed on the side in the same cursive font you might use to write "live, laugh, love." On my way, I passed some young people with interesting haircuts and an acoustic guitar. They were practicing a protest song.

There's an earnestness to rallies that claws at your heart. They are about anger, yes, but they're also about optimism—otherwise, why not be angry at home?—and optimism feels to me like the very tenderest underbelly you can show. The unspoken assumption of a protest is that someone is *listening*, someone is seeing and counting and registering your rage. A rally is an act of prayer. And like any other act of prayer, it requires a sort of unguarded hopefulness that is at once stubborn and naive and painfully vulnerable. You have to want something so much that you begin to believe it's possible, and that belief becomes a soft new organ that hurts even more when it dies. It's the same desperate idealism that lets people choose to have kids, thus giving themselves a million new things to grieve. Faith is a blister that grows on a spot rubbed raw. It's so easily punctured.

Inside the lightly frosted glass of the StoryCorps booth is a smaller red box, like the pulp inside a tooth. That's where Grammy had sat eleven years before, talking about the choice she made but didn't make, the choice that didn't feel like a choice. My grandmother believed in progress, reveled in it. She was fond of exclaiming in delight "America!" when faced with some new innovation or technology, even if she had no intention of using or even remembering it. (This was a joke. Her parents were immigrants, but she was born in the Bronx.) It's hard for me to imagine how she would react to *Roe v. Wade* being in danger, because it was so incomprehensible to her to go backwards. A few months before she died, she told me that at least nobody would admit to being an anti-Semite anymore; Hitler had just made it too *embarrassing*. It was 2017. If your strongest beliefs are where you're most vulnerable, what would it have done to her to see us dragged back into the bloody past? It felt, looking at the closed-up booth, as if she might still be in there, talking. What could I say to her, if she came out, about why I'm here, about where this is all going? With the brain God gave you, how can you believe it will get better? How can you go on?

The world is too bad for any of us. It is far, far too bad for anyone new—and one of the ways it's bad is that we are expected to keep bringing new people into this terrible world, piling them up like a sacrificial pyre. Some of them will be the kindling, and some the meat, and some the flames. We are not supposed to opt them out of this sick ritual: that is considered murder, which is to say, it's cheating. They have to live long enough to be put to death.

If we think about this too hard, we will never have children. If we let it stand, we will have to. If we have to, we will come to hate them. We can't look at the world too long. We can't look away.

What can you do? What else are you supposed to do? Take out your eyes and charge.

COME BACK
TWICE AS HARD

H ERE ARE SOME OF THE WOMEN I'm supposed to hate: The ones who are thinner than me. The ones who are prettier than me. The ones who are more successful, who I am supposed to think are all either hacks or overrated or mercenary *Lean In* types or slept their way to the top. The ones who are my husband's exes, my exes' exes, my exes' current partners especially my ex-husband's new wife, any partners for all time of anyone I had a crush on who wasn't interested in me. All my husband's female friends, who I'm supposed to find suspicious. The 53 percent of white women who voted for Trump, obviously, but also the annoying Women's March pussy-hat-wearing #resist types, or the brash performative hot-girl leftists, or honestly why not both. I am, depending on who's making the suggestions, supposed to feel disdain either for the women who talk about dating too much or the ones who are too puritanical, the ones who have too much money or the ones who complain too much about capitalism, the ones who are too loud about social justice or the ones who are too complicit in their own oppression, the ones who apologize too much or the ones who want too much attention.

It's not only men, or the male-dominated culture, that would have me cultivate this list of enemies. Women, too, sometimes demand the appropriate contempts as a kind of purity test: write in the burn book, prove you can sit with us. (Even some supposed feminists encourage each other to scorn any woman who deals professionally in sex, or who was raised with the insistence that she was a boy.) But as with most manifestations of misogyny, the question isn't who's making the demands. The question is who benefits. Who is served by keeping women at odds with each other? What happens when we refuse?

❧

When I was very young, twenty and twenty-one, I had a boyfriend who had a wife. It wasn't the version of this story you've heard before; he lived with me and she lived in New Zealand, and their marriage was over in all but legal name. But they were still friends—we were all friends, in a low-level way. Every six months or so, we would put together a box of American candy for her—candy I thought was kind of trash, Sour Patch Kids and Altoids and Jelly Bellies, compared with the Jaffas and Mackintosh's toffees we got in return. But that's what she asked for, so that's what we sent. Once, on the phone, I said I was surprised about the kinds of candy Kiwis liked, and she said something I didn't quite catch, and at my request repeated "SAOW-WER CANE-DEE" in her idea of an American accent. I think about that a lot, even now. Anyway, that's the kind of friends we were: sour candy friends.

Aside from her candy preferences, I didn't know much about Jane. I only even vaguely knew what she looked like; he didn't have a lot of photos, and this was before it was easy to put pictures on the internet. (She had black hair and pale skin and black clothes and bangs, but we were goths so that described half of the women we knew.) But I knew she was mentally ill, and how, and to what degree, and what kinds of therapy she did for it, and how it had affected their marriage. All of his exes were mentally ill, Jane perhaps most of all, but at least she was working on it—not like the ex right before me, who I *had* met, before he and I were dating, before they broke up and she went (I was told) bugfuck crazy. The ex before her was Jane: borderline personality disorder, years of intensive therapy. The ex before *that* . . . well, he'd hit her once, and he felt terrible about it, and if he ever did it again, he'd kill himself. (He told me this while crying. Men love to cry when they tell you these things.) But yes, he probably wouldn't have done it if she weren't so nuts.

I kept tabs on some of the other crazy ex-girlfriends, out of curiosity— we both did, just to see how crazy they were. People didn't have Twitter back then, but they did have LiveJournals: pseudonymous but largely public diaries. That's how I found out that the woman he'd dated right before me, the one I'd been friendly with before she went off the rails, had learned she couldn't get pregnant, and was having a hard time with it emotionally. Someone had responded to this with anonymous nasty comments about her infertility and why she deserved it. I didn't know who did it, but she had a guess: she emailed my boyfriend accusing him.

They'd had a chilly relationship since their breakup, but he did her the favor of telling her who he thought the real culprit was. "It must have been Jane," he wrote back. "You know how she is." Of course she knew. Every one of his girlfriends knew how every previous one was. We all thought, for a little while, that we would be the first one who wasn't.

I don't know which fight eventually drove me to talk to Jane. She had always been kind to me, but in a distant way—and not just due to the thousands of miles between us, which mattered more in those days, even on the internet. And for my part, though I liked her, I didn't entirely trust her. In my understanding, her mental illness was something she was wrestling with daily; she didn't have the bandwidth to be a supportive friend. And besides, from what he told me, she was unpredictable and often took things personally to the point of meltdown—poor qualities in a confidante. Anyway, it wasn't as if fights were unusual enough to be worth remarking on. There were a lot of accusations in that relationship, a lot of sulking, a lot of silent seething while I tried to figure out what I'd done wrong. There were a lot of nights when I would try to go to bed, only to find he'd put my pillows out in the hall and locked the door.

For the sake of argument, though, let's say it was the time I asked him for a quarter. He'd been unemployed for much of the year we'd been together; he'd moved to DC for a job, but quit when the leadership turned out to be too hard to deal with, and then gotten another job and quit that too. He'd had the idea that he would instead get rich selling weight-loss products for a multilevel marketing scheme, and spent several hundred dollars on stock before giving that up too. Now, he wanted to get a certification in entry-level computer technology, while I continued paying the rent. (I had been working three part-time jobs, mostly retail, when we started living together, although I'd left some of them to finish my senior year of college.) I had asked whether perhaps he could study for the certification while also holding a job. He hadn't taken that well.

Anyway, we went to 7-Eleven so he could buy cigarettes (Camel Lights, all DC goths smoke Camel Lights), and I grabbed something too, probably an ice cream bar. It cost a little over an even dollar amount, so I asked if he had a quarter so I could get less loose change. He stared at me in naked fury, spat out, "Just because I don't have a job doesn't mean I'm *helpless*," and stalked out of the store. I was half a block behind him the whole way home. He never looked back.

I did not and, indeed, still don't understand what really happened that day. I was angry at him (a little) and ashamed of making him angry at me (a lot), but even more than that, I was completely baffled. When I begged for him to clarify what I'd done to make him so mad, he described more or less the encounter I remembered—I asked for a quarter, he told me he wasn't helpless, he stormed away. In his mind, the insult was obvious, the response proportional and relevant. Often in the aftermath of our fights, he'd tell me about ways I'd slighted him that I didn't even remember, but not this time. I seemed to accurately recall what had infuriated him, I just didn't understand *why*.

So this may have been why I finally turned to Jane—to blow off steam, but also to see if she could tell me what I'd done wrong. I suppose I expected her to say something like, "You know, he just has so much pride." That was certainly what I was used to: stepping carefully around his pride and all his pet resentments.

I don't remember verbatim what she said, but it wasn't that. What I do remember is that she'd clearly been waiting for me to ask. *This is just who he is*, she told me. *You're just seeing him clearly now.* She was gentle with me about it but also palpably relieved. *He's always been this person: angry, bitter, casting about for someone to blame, landing every time on the person closest to hand. He always will be. He isn't your fault and he isn't going to change.*

Our computers were catty-corner in our awful dining room/office. (Grey-beige rental carpet, card table, stereo system, mismatched particle-board desks, KMFDM posters taped to the walls. I was in college; he was in his thirties.) I was suddenly aware of how visible my screen was, how angry he would be if he knew I'd turned to her for advice. And I realized: This is why I wasn't supposed to get close to her. This is why we were supposed to view each other with suspicion. Men keep women at odds with each other so we won't tell each other what we know.

He had not, as far as I know, exactly *lied* about her. She had in fact been diagnosed with borderline personality disorder, and had done a lot of hard emotional work to cope with anxieties and intrusive thoughts. She talked frankly about these things. He hadn't made them up; he'd just used them against her.

I say he hadn't lied about her. That's not exactly true. Those nasty, taunting messages about infertility, supposedly left by his "crazy" ex-wife to torment his "crazy" ex-girlfriend? I don't have to tell you, do I? You already knew. The more the women in his life were isolated from each other, even turned against each other, the safer he was: safe from blame, safe from consequence, safe from self-reflection. He was breeding a stable of scapegoats.

～

The Hydra was created to bring down a man. The goddess Hera raised the monster as a weapon to use against one of her husband Zeus's many illegitimate sons. First she sent serpents to kill the child, then called Alcides, but the infant throttled them before they could attack. His parents (or anyway, his mother and her husband) changed the boy's name to Heracles, "glory of Hera," in an attempt to placate the goddess—but by this time, her wrath was entrenched. And she was already thinking bigger than single snakes.

The Hydra, the creature Hera reared to take Heracles down, was a snake taken to exponential extremes: a giant water serpent with nine heads (or in some tellings, fifty or a hundred). A nest of vipers, in the form of a single creature. Of course Hera—proud, jealous, vengeful, the ancient archetype of the petty, suspicious wife—would make use of such a minion. (Never mind that Hera's spite, while generally misdirected, was always righteous; setting snakes on a baby is a poor way to handle marital conflict, but Zeus *was* cheating on her. Again.)

Heracles took on the Hydra as one of the tasks he was required to perform to expiate the crime of killing his wife and children. (Arguably, it worked. You probably remember the "labors of Hercules," the Roman version of Heracles; you probably don't remember the murder. It wasn't in the Disney movie *or* the Kevin Sorbo show.) The killing was Hera's fault, too—she had caused his mad rampage—but he still had to burn off the sin, in the form of a series of apparently impossible assignments from a cowardly king. The first labor was killing the fearsome Nemean lion, invulnerable to weapons, which Heracles wrestled down with his demigod strength and skinned with its own adamantine claws. The hero wore its impenetrable skin wrapped around him when he went to meet the Hydra, like a nigh-invulnerable hoodie. With his "pitiless bronze sword," according to Hesiod, or with his club according to Pseudo-Apollodorus, Heracles started to lop off (or knock in) the creature's heads. But for every one he severed, two more grew. Having slashed his way through all nine necks, Heracles found himself faced with an eighteen-headed creature. The more he fought it, the stronger it became.

What do you do when bashing away at your foe doesn't seem to weaken it? For the first and last time in his labors, Heracles had to call for help. His cousin Iolaus stepped in with a burning torch or brand, to cauterize each neck after it was severed. The two men, working together, defeated a creature that was too much for the hero alone.

What makes the Hydra a threat is that she cannot be diminished. The Nemean lion seemed invincible because of its blade-proof hide, but that just necessitates a change in approach; once Heracles gave up on weapons, he handily wrestled it down. The Hydra, though, thrives on damage. In Ovid's *Heroides*, structured as letters between classical heroes and the women they left behind, Heracles's wife, Deianira, calls her "the fertile serpent that sprang forth again from the fruitful wound, grown rich from her own hurt."

It's not hard to kill a monster if you're Heracles, a monster killer from birth. The snakes he killed in his cradle were strangled with his bare hands. So was the Nemean lion, labor one, after he bashed it with a club. The club is also how he dispatched with the two-headed dog who guarded the flock of cattle he stole for his tenth labor. The Stymphalian birds, labor six, he killed with arrows. He even managed to overpower Cerberus, the three-headed canine guard of the Gates of Hell. When you have the super strength, when you have the club, who's going to stop you?

But a creature that feeds on the fight, a creature that comes back stronger with every wound: such a creature can, at least, give you a run for your money. Heracles does eventually defeat the Hydra, but not easily, and not alone. To dispatch the multiheaded, constantly regenerating female monster, the man who hugged a lion to death needs a wingman wielding fire. And even then, she has her revenge.

❧

Even with women I like, women I rely on, I've adopted the language of conflict and animosity. When my friend Helena writes something good, which is to say any time she writes something, I inevitably text her a string of invective with no preamble: "fuck you, how dare you, I hate you, I hate this." She does the same to me. I've had jokingly abusive friendships with men before; one dear friend and I developed a formula for fresh new horrible insults so we could avoid stagnation. (It's body part or secretion plus animal, if you want to play along!) Another flips me double birds every time I walk into a room even if he's holding his own infant child. But there is no deeper truth in these aggressions—the joy is the pure joy of yelling. With Helena, there is a tiny seed of reality: not that I hate her or hate her writing, but that I love it so much that I feel genuinely angry. That, essentially, it makes me hate myself for not measuring up.

I've noticed the same love-by-way-of-hate construction from other women talking about women. "She's a willowy blond goddess who wears no makeup and doesn't care about clothing," one friend recently texted me about an in-law, who is also an accomplished scholar. "AND she writes thank you notes, AND she's so nice and super funny and has the perfect twisted streak. I ducking hate her." Autocorrect leapt in to soften the punchline a little bit, but the sentiment is clear: anything we admire or envy, up to and including being a genuinely wonderful person we truly love, is something that on some level we ducking hate.

This comes partly from competition, from the *Highlander* rules so often imposed on women: there can be only one. Like the Hydra, the immortals in *Highlander* can only be killed by decapitation. You can get them with one good blow, though, which makes them substantially more vulnerable than the Hydra. (Although now that I'm thinking about it, who says the Hydra *must* be decapitated? Could Heracles have poisoned her, or pushed her off a cliff, or waited for her to die of old age? It doesn't really matter, since he didn't try. Anyway, these approaches don't work for the *Highlander* immortals.) When murdered, instead of regenerating, they impart their life force to the killer. Eventually, the plot goes, the last man standing will have access to wonderful power. Perhaps some unconscious part of me believes Helena and I are in contention for a closely guarded single slot. Like if we keep climbing, and outdoing all challengers, and absorbing each other's life force, we'll eventually achieve the level of "woman essayist men talk about to prove they've read a woman essayist." There can be only one Joan Didion.

Even more than competition against other women, though, our paradoxical conflict with the people we most admire comes from the way all women are pitted against an ideal. Other women's success on those metrics feels like a referendum, in a way men's success does not. "She's perfect and I ducking hate her" is shorthand for "I'm not perfect and I ducking hate myself."

This drive to hate each other (or say we hate each other, meaning we are disappointed in ourselves) is not exactly inborn. Of course there are fundamentally mean people of every gender, but the jokes about women finding new BFFs in every bar bathroom, or flipping out over their friends' hot photos in a way men rarely even try to achieve, aren't just jokes. I think most women earnestly love cheerleading for other women. (I also think men and nonbinary people love this! And men would love it more if they didn't get so many messages that supportiveness counts as an emotion and is therefore uncool.) It just *feels* better to admire people than to envy or disdain them. So when we turn so easily against each other—either sincerely, or as a way of covertly turning against ourselves—we are not doing it on instinct. We're following a cultural pattern.

Laurie Penny, undoubtedly one of the women I am supposed to hate—she's thinner, younger, *and* more successful than me—has published a lengthy essay about some of the reasons behind this pattern, the reasons that a male-dominated society encourages and rewards female competition. In the *Baffler* magazine, she writes:

> Women and girls are expected to compete for male attention on a professional and social level as well as on the spectrum that runs from makeouts to marriage. In both cases, the suspicion of scarcity makes the competition desperate: there are only so many places in the world for talented people who happen to be female. Men in positions of social power—within a workplace, a friendship group, a family—make women jockey for their attention, sometimes instinctively, without even noticing. You have to win on the terms that patriarchy has laid out to ensure women are always battling themselves and each other: you have to win the girl game. What that girl game is changes as you get older, but it's always about being good enough. It's about being pretty enough, skinny enough, popular enough, cool enough, desired by men even if men are not what you yourself desire. Soon it will also be about having the perfect relationship, the perfect marriage, the perfect family; being able to balance your home and work life without being visibly exhausted. You will be invited, constantly, to compare yourself to other women and only to other women on each and every one of these axes.

The intention of keeping women pitted against each other for limited resources, in other words, is to keep us from noticing how limited the resources are. But it serves a dual purpose: it also keeps us from comparing notes. Like an abuser who isolates you from your support network, a culture with an anti-woman bent has a vested interest in cutting us off from outside perspectives, denying us the external reality checks that might reveal the whole thing as a scam. If you find your female coworkers threatening, you never find out if you're all having the same experiences of unfair pay or sexual harassment. If you sneer at your partner's exes, it takes you that much longer to realize the problem is him, not you.

"The Best Girl game . . . is a competition with no winners," Penny writes. But as usual, there are winners. They're just men.

❧

At 6 p.m. on October 11, 2017, I got a text from a friend reading "well, hello there." Attached was a link to a Google doc called "Shitty Media Men."

I was walking home from work and it was difficult to read the spreadsheet on my phone. I could see that it was a list of names, affiliations, and alleged infractions, ranging from suggestive messages to rape, but it was impossible to see the name and the accusation at the same time. Still, it was clear enough what I was looking at. "Yes," I texted back. "We need this."

When I got home, I perused the list at length. I saw plenty of names that meant nothing to me, but others I knew: bylines I recognized, former coworkers, people I'd heard stories about. Some were surprises, but many were not. A number of entries were highlighted in red: men who stood accused by multiple women of physical sexual violence. It was a whisper network made manifest, years' and careers' worth of quiet warnings in digital compendium form. At the top, it read "Please never name an accuser, and please never share this document with a man."

The list came at a time when many women felt we especially needed a collected set of protective whispers. Less than a week earlier, the *New York Times* had broken an explosive story about film producer Harvey Weinstein's decades of invasive sexual overtures toward women in his orbit—often by hosting "professional" meetings in his hotel room, in a bathrobe, and offering a massage—and threatening or paying off those who complained. An article in the *New Yorker* on October 10 added more detail to the Weinstein accusations, including charges of rape, and further reporting deepened the allegations in ways that would have been hard to believe if they weren't so easy to believe. In all, more than sixty women said they'd experienced harassment or assault at Weinstein's hands.

I don't know what men experienced when they read these revelations. I know what women, and people raised women, saw: all the ignorers and enablers, everyone who said "he's not so bad" or "you just have to know how to handle him" or "can't you get past it, just for now, just for this, just for me." We saw, too, the women who had raised alarms, who had said "watch out for that one" or even "I'm not leaving you alone with him."

"You Can't Get Away with This Shit Anymore" read a headline on *The Awl*, a day after the *New Yorker* piece:

> The explosive Weinstein accusations have opened all kinds of flood-gates, men and women everywhere are coming forward with their own stories. Every industry from food service to the art world to the field of Antarctic geology has its own Harvey Weinstein, and we're not keeping quiet about it anymore. So let this serve not a vague threat but rather an explicit notice: the whisper networks have officially become shouting conference calls. Our truth is that your power is no longer as great as you think it is. It's not over exactly, but everything is different now.

The spreadsheet started later that day. It felt like a distillation of that promise: that things would be different, that we wouldn't keep quiet, that they wouldn't get away with it anymore. The women who contributed to the list had been keeping these experiences to themselves, or near enough: telling their friends over drinks, maybe pulling aside a new employee or young freelancer and letting her know how shit was, but never taking the dangerous and vulnerable and likely futile step of making a public accusation. Now, the stuff "everyone knew"—which everyone never knew, or else everyone would have been safe—was in a format where everyone could see it.

By that evening I'd gotten the spreadsheet from two other friends. Then it disappeared. "Too big, too fast," someone said. "The owners got spooked." The next morning, there was an article on *BuzzFeed News*:

"What to Do with 'Shitty Media Men'?" In case the punctuation isn't clear there, the question wasn't what to do about the men. It was what to do about the document.

"Things do get complicated when you start lumping all of this behavior together in a big anonymous spreadsheet of unsubstantiated allegations against dozens of named men—who were not given the chance to respond," wrote Doree Shafrir, a *BuzzFeed News* staffer with five colleagues and three former colleagues on the list. She went on to acknowledge that women are rarely empowered to make such accusations personally or publicly, and that we are forced to protect one another in secret due to a culture in which "our motives are suspect, our reputations are maligned, our victimhood called into question." But the buzzwords had been dropped: "unsubstantiated," "anonymous," "not given a chance to respond."

Once the secret was out, tweets and articles followed—many from women—scolding the "gossips" and hand-wringing over the one-sidedness of the stories. This is the danger when the network of woman-to-woman whispers is given shape and put out into the world. It can be hauled up for questioning and found to suffer from too little input from men.

Here's the thing, though: the list worked. Not flawlessly—some multiply accused men went unscathed, and it's possible that some of the dubious honorees didn't deserve to be on such a list at all. But in the subsequent months, three known bad actors, people who had been warned about in real-life whisper networks for years but never faced consequences, were fired from or quit their jobs. The *Atlantic* dropped contributing editor Leon Wieseltier, formerly of the *New Republic*, in October. *BuzzFeed News* fired one of its listed employees, White House correspondent Adrian Carrasquillo, in November. In December, *Paris Review* editor Lorin Stein stepped down during an investigation, and the magazine subsequently replaced him with a woman. They weren't exactly dropping like flies, but at roughly one a month, they were dropping like uterine linings.

Stories about all of these men had been circulating throughout their careers, even sometimes reaching the mainstream, albeit twisted into praise. In a 2011 *New York Times* profile of Stein, he offers to "pimp out" author Zadie Smith, and jokes about how many people he kissed at a literary party. But women had mostly talked about them quietly, two and three at a time. The mathematics that finally brought them down was the exponential spread of the spreadsheet: two, then four, then sixteen, and on and on.

In early January, three months after the list made its rounds, the second-order whisper network surrounding the list activated again. I got a message from a friend saying that *Harper's Magazine* was planning to run a piece by a known antifeminist, outing the list's creator, Moira Donegan. Instead, Donegan broke the news herself the next day in the *Cut, New York Magazine*'s women's-interest site. In her powerful essay unmasking herself, Donegan was candid about the flaws in her undertaking—"I was incredibly naive when I made the spreadsheet," she wrote—but she also talked about the purpose it had served:

> Watching the cells populate, it rapidly became clear that many of us had weathered more than we had been willing to admit to one another. There was the sense that the capacity for honesty, long suppressed, had finally been unleashed. This solidarity was thrilling, but the stories were devastating. I realized that the behavior of a few men I had wanted women to be warned about was far more common than I had ever imagined. This is what shocked me about the spreadsheet: the realization of how badly it was needed, how much more common the experience of sexual harassment or assault is than the opportunity to speak about it.

We need that opportunity, to compare notes and find common experiences and come to one another's defense, about many aspects of life under patriarchy, not just sexual harassment. And all of these divisive strategies—making women suspicious of each other, training us to compete or judge or take each other down, keeping us ashamed of openly talking about what's happened to us, clutching your pearls or shouting or threatening when we do—are methods of avoiding or undermining exactly this need. (There was plenty of shouting and threatening in the wake of the list, in particular a midlist writer who filed an unsuccessful lawsuit against Donegan, alleging that inclusion on the list was the sole reason his latest novel wasn't more successful. Notably, he tried to demand the identities of every woman who had added to or even shared the list, so he could sue them too.)

There is power in talking to each other, in protecting each other, in hearing each other's grievances, both when they do and don't match with our own. The fact that they want to cut us off, cauterize us, set us against each other: this is all we need to know that our power will come from alliance.

Heracles did kill the Hydra, but in the end that didn't go too well for him—he wound up having to do an extra task because he had help. (Men, even more than women, are trained into self-defeating solitude.) On the plus side, he was able to dip his arrows in the Hydra's powerful venom, rendering them extra deadly. That helped him out with two of his other labors, so on the whole he was ahead, until the centaur Nessus tried to kidnap and rape his wife.

Centaurs, being half-horse, are fast. Heracles was faster: he shot Nessus through the chest with one of his Hydra-fied arrows while the centaur was trying to carry Deianira across the river. But neither arrows nor venom guarantee an instant death. Nessus, who knew that the potent Hydra gall would taint his blood, had just enough time to lay a trap. He promised Deianira that his blood was a powerful love potion that would ensure her husband's fidelity.

In fact, Heracles was kind of a dog. He had mistresses and children all over the place, as seemed to be the due of a hero. Deianira had been putting up with this with the equanimity expected of wives at the time, but it really rankled when he started to woo Iole, a woman from his past. Before he and Deianira married, Heracles had hoped to wed Iole, and even won a contest for her hand—but her father had forbidden it, and Deianira was his second choice. (Of all the current-partner's-exes you're supposed to hate, the one you suspect they're still carrying a torch for is probably Enemy Number One.) Deianira feared losing her man, but she had a secret weapon: she soaked a shirt in the centaur's poisoned blood and sent it to her husband as a gift. When Heracles put it on, it started to burn him so badly that he built his own funeral pyre, threw himself into the fire, and died.

This is a sad story, however you read it—the hero brought down by an error, the wife whose jealousy makes her lose her husband forever. But I can't help a secret smile at the way the Hydra strikes out at abusers from beyond the grave: first the rapist, then the philanderer. Cut off her head, and a fresh one comes in to bite you, and brings a friend. Gang up to destroy her, and she'll poison your life. Sliced and seared and diluted, the Hydra is still bringing men down.

❧

Solidarity is, in many ways, a doomed enterprise. For starters, most people aren't that great, although it's not impossible to rise above this. You don't have to like someone to believe they should have rights. More challenging are the effects of intersecting oppressions and white privilege. The people least in need of shoring up are always loudly scolding those who need it most.

The idea behind intersectionality, coined and defined by scholar Kimberlé Crenshaw, is that different forms of marginalization overlap and intensify one another; a black woman, for instance, is simply not experiencing the same kind of sexism as a white woman, because she is experiencing sexism that intersects with racism. The two are not separate, or even uncomplicatedly additive. Class, disability, sexuality, and other areas of potential oppression also overlap—or maybe it's more accurate to say they weave together, since "overlap" implies they can be pulled apart. Intersecting oppressions aren't a quilt over a blanket. They're a yellow warp of sexism and a blue weft of racism mingling to form green. Crenshaw, who is a lawyer among her other accomplishments, has cited a case in which five black women sued General Motors for "race and gender discrimination." They struggled to prove their suit because the law considered it two separate claims—race discrimination and gender discrimination. Not all the women at GM were discriminated against, just the black ones, and not all the black employees were discriminated against, just the women. Therefore, legally, there was no race or gender discrimination. Put like that, any approach besides intersectionality seems absurd.

The existence of multiple areas of oppression does not, on its own, make solidarity impossible. It just requires us to power up empathy, recognizing that other people's needs and experiences may be both valid and different from our own. The problem is that the fewer overlapping oppressions you're burdened with, the more power you tend to have, and the less you tend to empathize with or even recognize the needs of others. This is generally ignorant rather than malicious, at least at first: it's astonishingly easy simply not to grasp difficult realities you've never had to face. (The more I try to live day to day in a crumbling civilization on a dying planet, the more I'm convinced that this mental instinct is *supposed* to be self-protective.) But it leads to whole movements—including feminism, for a long time and in many ways still—being built as though injustices happen in isolation and can be picked off one by one. To the people with the most power and the loudest voices, generally, they do. Everyone else is left wondering when their fight will come—or just having the fight on their own. (Much of the great work of modern feminism has been thanks to the labor of women of color, despite the fact that they've been perpetually underserved.)

Mikki Kendall's #SolidarityIsForWhiteWomen hashtag, and related hashtags around the same time in 2013, attempted to collect and distill this idea: that calls for "supporting your sisters," or whatever, conceal the fact that high-visibility feminism centers and elevates white women. "[W]hite feminism has argued that gender should trump race since its inception," Kendall wrote in the *Guardian*. "That rhetoric not only erases the experiences of women of color, but also alienates many from a movement that claims to want equality for all." Race and other intersections can't be secondary concerns. We can't aim for women's solidarity first, and address racism second, because to do so means solidarity is only achievable by people who aren't also experiencing racism.

I'm aware of the pitfalls of seeming to say, as a white woman no less, that we are all part of the same creature. It implies so much commonality: a single skeleton, a single heart. How can this be true when we don't start from the same place, don't experience the same pressures, don't have access to the same resources? But the true monstrousness, and thus the true strength, of the Hydra is not her shared body, but her ability to take a hit and bite back twofold. We may not collectively *be* a Hydra, a single animal with many heads. But we can emulate the Hydra, the particular kind of monstrous heroism that comes from being undiminishable. The recognition that our lives are far from identical is part of the project; it allows us to step in where others are cut down or bashed in or weak. Our task is not to share a heart but to share a goal, where the goal is liberation. Our great strength, if we can use it, is that we cannot be completely destroyed—that whatever angle we're attacked from, there will always be more of us, riled up and righteous and coming back twice as hard.

The hundred heads of the Hydra rustle and whisper together. They may not cherish their neighbors, who snipe at each other or slow everyone down by showboating or drag behind in protest and have to be lugged along. They may nurse grievances against each other, from small resentments to massively incompatible morals. They may not understand each other. But two hundred eyes, or near enough, still turn in the end towards a mutual goal: to live, to move forward, to resist attack, to grow instead of diminish. To double in strength with every strike instead of striking at ourselves. To surge with a poison so strong that our pain alone can kill an enemy. To know who the enemy is.

MOTHER OF MONSTERS

MANY OF THE MONSTERS in this book are family. Scylla, Chimera, the Hydra, and the Sphinx, at least according to some chroniclers, are sisters; so is the original Gorgon, the mother of Medusa. The Harpies, in one story, are at least their half-siblings. They are also kin to the three-headed dog Cerberus, who guards the underworld; the iron-skinned Nemean lion; and the eagle who perpetually eats the liver of Prometheus, creator of humans, as punishment for stealing fire from the gods. The mother of all these creatures is Echidna, and, as is fitting for the mother of monsters, she is also a monster herself: a woman to the waist, a snake below.

Echidna lived in hiding. Born in a cave, she birthed her children in a cave, and then retreated with them to a cave (or possibly to the underworld prison-pit Tartarus) after her mate Typhon challenged Zeus, king of gods, and was defeated. Typhon, a hundred-headed winged giant with snakes for legs, wound up trapped under what is now Mount Etna. The danger in fighting a god is that he might put a mountain on you. And Echidna, born in darkness, never really out of darkness, went further underground in fear of vengeance. "Echidna, his hideous mate, escaped destruction," says my beloved childhood volume *D'Aulaires' Book of Greek Myths*. "She cowered in a cave, protecting Typhon's dreadful offspring, and Zeus let them live as a challenge to future heroes."

Technically, Echidna's story is a footnote to Typhon's. He fought for supremacy against the gods; she only bore his children. But *D'Aulaires'* illustrates this moment—Typhon's hubris, defeat, and imprisonment in a volcano—with a half-page, full-color illustration of Echidna. She huddles with her horrible children under a canopy of stalactites, her hair as elaborately curled as a classical statue's, her snake tail studded with inflamed pinkish dots that look like nipples or sores. The spiky rock walls cup her gently and closely as a Labrador's mouth. Green-skinned and red-eyed, she grimaces and peers around her small cell, arms reached out to protectively cradle the baby monstrosities she suckles. All her children are depicted in cuddly baby form: a puppy-faced Nemean lion, a Sphinx with stubby immature wings. They are all she has. They will grow to strike fear in the hearts of men.

❧

I think a lot about shame, about the way it's shaped me. What would my life be like if I wasn't fundamentally ashamed of myself, if I hadn't been ashamed of everything about myself for as long as I can remember? It's almost impossible to imagine. So many of my choices have been animated by the desire to hide or apologize. The shame-free version of me would have gone to school differently, traveled differently, dated differently, lived differently, worked differently, written this book differently.

It's hard to identify the source of this shame, because it's lived with me so long. The proximal causes are often absurd on their face. A few years ago I tried to keep track, for a few days, of every thought that made me so seized with shame that I would curse at myself out loud. Here is a selection:

- *Remembered that two nights ago I didn't understand the taxi driver the first time*
- *Sang a karaoke song and did fine*
- *Remembered that last night I had been unable to immediately find the hand soap in someone else's bathroom*
- *Composed a few lines of a story in my head even though I know I can't write fiction*

- *Remembered that three days ago I said something about a parent to someone who's lost a parent*
- *Ate too much bread*
- *Remembered that a year and a half ago I slept with someone who I thought was nice but they weren't*
- *Got sweaty after hot yoga*
- *Got a compliment and awkwardly tried to credit other people who deserved it more*
- *Was slightly confused about meeting scheduling*
- *Misremembered whether a Star Trek episode was The Original Series or The Next Generation, neither of which I've watched*
- *Bought a lipstick last month*

All of these are just the raw nerve endings connected to larger bundles of remorse, of course. I am ashamed of not being prettier, more physically and socially graceful, more successful, more talented, smarter, nicer to be around. I am ashamed of having needs, hungers, smells, exudations, stumbles, misconceptions, ambitions that shade perhaps into delusions. I am, in short, ashamed of every way I impinge on others, every way I overstep the bounds of what I'm supposed to be.

When you are marked by shame, and by its attendant self-hatred and fear, you carry it with you like a parasitic twin—riding coiled heavily around your stomach, snaking out a hand to cover your mouth, to yank down your hemline, to swat people away. It chooses your food, your clothes, your words; it ventriloquizes you, snatching your phone to text "no thanks, I can't" or "me? I'm fine." It croaks in your ear when you try to sleep. You become a hybrid creature: half woman, half shame.

It's all very well to talk about the power of monsters, the heroism of monsters. But being a monster doesn't always feel powerful. Sometimes it feels like being twisted and warped, annealed against your will to a malignant shadow. Sometimes it feels like retreating into a cave with the wrongs you've created, dragging the slithering bulk of self-loathing behind you.

Wouldn't it be easy if we were always joyful horrors, iron fangs and wings as wide as freedom, stepping on a man's heart with one delicate taloned paw? If we understood our monstrousness as heroic, understood it with such sun-bright clarity that other people's doubt would crumble before us? Maybe that's possible for somebody, somewhere—but she probably doesn't read the news, or go on Twitter, or try to date men, and she maybe does a lot of drugs. For most of us, no matter how hard you work to truly believe that your aberrations are beautiful, some of the time—maybe most of the time—you will find yourself harrowed into submission, chased or retreating. That's just how the world is. One person's strength is rarely enough to withstand it.

This pain is not weakness. It's a rational response. Even when you know you are an expert, being condescended to makes you feel small. Even when you know your bodily autonomy is more important than any clump of cells, it's hurtful to be called a murderer or an incubator. Even when you can list off a hundred reasons why our culture valorizes thin bodies and why they're all bullshit, being told you're disgusting is breathtakingly harsh. It is painful to be dismissed, disenfranchised, misgendered, shouted down, dogpiled, mocked. These things hurt because they're supposed to—not because they have merit but because they are attacks.

But even the snake in her hole, even the pockmarked and cowering creature, even the woman so tightly yoked to her shame that she no longer knows which one of them is the parasite, can bring something ferocious and valiant into the world. It may not feel good, but then again, birth never does.

❧

When stories describe the birth of monsters, which they rarely do, it tends to be cataclysmic: the baby phoenix fledged from its own cremation, or Pegasus springing from Medusa's still-spouting stump. The monsters of myth are created in blood and fire, or born offstage. Go figure that the men who told the stories didn't want to dwell on the realities of gestation and labor—which, yes, tend to involve blood, but also shit and sweat and tears.

Which means it is up to us to decide: What does it mean to be pregnant with monstrosity? How are monsters delivered? What do they feed on, in their vulnerable infancy? If the monster represents difference and deviation, if they lurk just beyond the border of what's allowed, then they must—like shame—be generated by stepping over our bounds. We swell up with shame, fertilized by all the expectations thrust upon us: the expectation to be small, to be pretty, to be pristine and calm and simple and undemanding and just stupid enough not to seem like a challenge. Monsters are created in the difference between what we are supposed to be and what we are.

Gravid with everything that's wrong with us, our instinct is to hide, a sort of permanent confinement. But what if we labored, instead, to nurture all these deviations, all these insufficiencies—to rear them into viable creatures and send them out into the world? A swarm of little Too-Muches—too ugly, too needy, too arrogant, too angry, too strange. Even when we're frightened, even when we want to hide, we can rear these hideous children to outlive us.

We are expected to be mothers, but not like this: not midwives to our mistakes. But we are through with expectation.

In her knurled womb of stone, Echidna reaches out to protect and comfort her little aberrations. "Zeus let them live as a challenge for future heroes," my *D'Aulaires'* says—a casual death sentence. These just-born creatures are predestined from birth to be battled and defeated. They will never be heroes; their deaths will be the feats the heroes achieve.

Part of the exhaustion of being a monster, part of what keeps you at home in your cave, is knowing that it's a foregone conclusion: Everything you create will be attacked and destroyed. Everything will *exist* for being attacked and destroyed, and for heroes to be made in the destroying of it. All your monstrous progeny, so painfully birthed: they will never come to anything but cannon fodder. It is so hard to live beyond boundaries when you know the consequences. Who can bring children into the world knowing they're fated to be killed? Who wants to go through the pain of birth only to roll right into the pain of grief?

But the stories we're given can be rewritten, reconceived, even redacted—and nobody redacts like a monster. Imagine tending your terrible children until they're strong enough not only to leave the cave, but to rip out the heart of the story. Imagine nurturing them until their little claws grow sharp enough to shred the old sentiments, the old sentences. Imagine: "Zeus let them live as . . . future heroes."

❧

There's a version of feminism—or maybe, dated as it is, it would be more accurately called "women's lib"—that celebrates femininity as fundamentally yoked to birth. Women, we are supposed to believe, are special because they are life-givers. The womb is the resting place of the sacred feminine, the generative power that sets us apart.

This is silly, for a number of reasons. (Infertile women. Women who've had hysterectomies. Women assigned male at birth, or otherwise born without a uterus. Women who think it's not *actually* that feminist to be told that the most valuable thing about them is their reproductive organs.) But our capacity for birthing monsters really is one of our greatest weapons. You don't need any special equipment for this; monsters are engendered in the act of eating or fucking or shouting, of aspiring above your so-called station, of living in a body without shame. The tighter our constraints, the more they pour from us every time we overflow: a seed bursting open. Like Echidna, we make a womb out of our cell.

This, in the end, is what matters: not that we stand proudly in all our monstrousness every day but that we find small ways to gestate dissent and deviation, to nurse and nurture the things that are supposed to be wrong with us until they grow into something great. This is our strength: that each of us has the capacity to be not only a monster but a mother of monsters. We can birth from our own bodies every one of men's worst fears.

ACKNOWLEDGMENTS

THANK YOU to Nikki Chung, my editor at *Catapult*, who took a chance on this weird idea for an essay series at a time when I had given up hope that anyone would agree with me that there was a book in it. You are an extraordinary person, and I am so lucky to be your friend and fan.

Thank you to my agent, Beth Vesel, who reached out after reading one of those *Catapult* essays and confirmed my suspicion, or at least participated in a folie à deux with me, that this was a book after all. Thank you also to her former assistant Marie Michels (now at Park & Fine), who was crucial in shaping the proposal and supporting me throughout the query process.

Thank you to Rakia Clark, my first editor at Beacon, who helped to hone my thinking about the project, and to Helene Atwan and Haley Lynch, who took up the torch when Rakia moved to HMH. It is an unexpected privilege to work closely with someone who genuinely loves your work, and while it's also a little nerve-racking—*shouldn't there be more criticism???*—Haley made it an unmitigated blessing. I cannot thank world-class copy editor Emily Dolbear enough for her crucial correcting and polishing, overseen by Beacon managing editor Susan Lumenello. Thank you to my brilliant illustrator, Samira Ingold, who saw intuitively into the hearts of these monsters and reflected them on the page. Thank you to production director Marcy Barnes, ever-patient and talented cover designer Carol Chu, and the rest of the production and design departments for making this book into a beautiful physical thing, and to Emily Powers, Caitlin Meyer, and the marketing and publicity departments for taking it out into the world.

Thank you to early essay readers Jaime Greenring, Angela Chen, and Kea Krause for your attention and care. Thank you especially to my writing inner circle, Jaya Saxena and Helena Fitzgerald, whose cheese plates, tarot readings, and yelling about Aerosmith were truly invaluable. You make me a better writer and almost certainly a better person by your collaboration, except when you make me a worse person which is also fun. (And thank you to Matt and Thomas for, among other things, the grace with which you let us invade your homes.)

Thank you to Jo Lou, associate editor and my right hand at *Electric Literature*, whose dedication and conscientiousness keep the site functioning. Jo, more than anyone else, made it possible for me to write a book while also having a day job, but she's much more than backup—she's a sharp, forward-thinking editor, and I've been fortunate to have her as a colleague.

Thank you to Jordan Ginsberg at *Hazlitt*, who helped shape the essay that became the substrate of "Charybdis," even though I was VERY rude to him for taking a long time with it. Sorry! Thank you also to Scaachi Koul, who at *Hazlitt* did so much to make me a better writer, even though she is an infuriating amount younger than me and it's very unfair that I had so much to learn from her.

Thank you to Emily Hughes and Kate Harding for moral support and letting me Be a Huge Bitch for a Second; to Meredith Yayanos, the original harpy, for helping me walk in the path she blazed; to Sarah Kurchak for the full-hearted embrace of our particular bullshit; and to Helen Rosner for a million things, including reassurance, gossip, advice, title brainstorming, use of her Hulu password, and sending me every mythology meme she saw.

Thank you to Andrea Oh for wrangling my works cited into shape, to the Banff Centre for the beautifully silent office in which I spent a week quintupling my daily output, to all the students at *Electric Literature*'s Banff residency for being so engaged and enthusiastic even though I frequently abandoned them to hole up in said office, to Karl Steel and Brian Flota for help accessing scholarly resources, to Joe Howley for Greek translation assistance, to Alex Marshall and Andrew Janke for helping me maintain the fiction that I could have functioning human friendships while writing this, to Laura Passin for still being my friend after all these years despite listening to me whine through the events in "That's What You Think," and to my Peaches.

I would not have been a writer without my family—which is kind of a curse but mostly a spectacular piece of good fortune. I was privileged to have parents and grandparents who prioritized education and who offered moral and material support even when I was taking risks or, arguably, making huge mistakes. I was also lucky to have a mother who's taken nine books through the trade publishing labyrinth, which meant that no part of this process was ever a mystery to me. Thank you for making my life easier in ways I'll probably never fully appreciate, and thank you for *D'Aulaire's Book of Greek Myths*. Thank you also to my sister Sam, my brother-in-law Evan, and my nieces, who I still hope will grow up into a better world. Don't read any of this until you're at least fourteen.

And thank you to my husband, Justin, first and last and always. Writing a book like this means sometimes setting yourself adrift; thank you for being my shore and my solid ground.

RESOURCES

GENERAL
Background works and works consulted across multiple chapters

Apollodorus. *The Library of Greek Mythology.* Translated by Keith Aldrich. Lawrence, KS: Coronado Press, 1975.

Apollonius Rhodius. *Argonautica.* Translated by William H. Race. Cambridge, MA: Harvard University Press, 2009.

Asma, Stephen T. *On Monsters: An Unnatural History of Our Worst Fears.* New York: Oxford University Press, 2009.

D'Aulaire, Ingri, and Edgar Parin D'Aulaire. *D'Aulaires' Book of Greek Myths.* New York: Delacorte Books for Young Readers, 1992.

Hesiod. *Theogony and Works and Days.* Translated by M. L. West. New York: Oxford University Press, 2008.

Homer. *The Odyssey.* Translated by Emily Wilson. New York: W. W. Norton & Company, 2017.

Hyginus. *The Myths of Hyginus.* Translated by Mary Grant. Lawrence: University of Kansas, 1960.

Murgatroyd, Paul. *Mythical Monsters in Classical Literature.* London: Bloomsbury Academic, 2013.

Ovid. *Metamorphoses.* Translated by Rolfe Humphries. Bloomington: Indiana University Press, 1971.

Smith, William, editor, *A Dictionary of Greek and Roman Biography and Mythology.* Boston: Little, Brown and Co., 1867.

Virgil, *The Aeneid.* Translated by Allen Mandelbaum. New York: Bantam Classic, 1981.

The following resources are organized by appearance within the chapter.

INTRODUCTION: SISTER MONSTERS
Met exhibit: Karoglou, Kiki. *Dangerous Beauty: Medusa in Classical Art.* New York: Metropolitan Museum of Art, 2018.

Grendel's mother: Menzer, Melinda J. "Aglaecwif ('Beowulf' 1259A): Implications for '-Wif' Compounds, Grendel's Mother, and Other 'Aglaecan.'" *English Language Notes* 34, no. 1 (September 1996): 1–6.

Cohen, Jeffrey Jerome, editor. *Monster Theory: Reading Culture.* Minneapolis: University of Minnesota Press, 1996.

HOW TO TURN A MAN TO STONE

Etymology of *monster*: *Oxford English Dictionary*. https://www.oed.com/viewdictionary entry/Entry/121738.

McFadden, Syreeta. "Teaching the Camera to See My Skin," *BuzzFeed News*, April 3, 2014. https://www.buzzfeednews.com/article/syreetamcfadden/teaching -the-camera-to-see-my-skin.

Cooper Jones, Chloé. "Such Perfection." *The Believer*, June 3, 2019. https://believer mag.com/such-perfection.

Eco, Umberto. "On the History of Ugliness," video lecture, University of Ljubljana. December 2007, Slovenia. http://videolectures.net/cd07_eco_thu.

Ugly laws: Henderson, Gretchen E. *Ugliness: A Cultural History*. London: Reaktion Books, 2015.

VORACIOUS

Onion, Rebecca. "How 'She Just Wants Attention' Became America's Hottest Sexist Insult." *Slate*, April 4, 2016. https://slate.com/human-interest/2016/04/how -she-just-wants-attention-became-americas-hottest-sexist-insult.html.

Honoratus, Maurus Servius. *Commentary on the Aeneid of Virgil*. Edited by Georg Thilo and Hermann Hagen. Leipzig: B.G. Teubner, 1881.

Gilmore, David D. *Misogyny: The Male Malady*. Philadelphia: University of Pennsylvania Press, 2003.

Minnesota starvation experiment: Kolata, Gina. *Rethinking Thin: The New Science of Weight Loss—and the Myths and Realities of Dieting*. New York: Picador, 2008.

DOGS BELOW THE WAIST

Hopman, Marianne Govers. *Scylla: Myth, Metaphor, Paradox*. Cambridge, UK: Cambridge University Press, 2016.

Ebenstein, Joanna. *The Anatomical Venus: Wax, God, Death & The Ecstatic*. London: Thames & Hudson, 2016.

King Lear hates vaginas: Shakespeare, William, *King Lear*. Edited by Russell Fraser. New York: Signet Classics, 1998.

Lewis, C. S. *The Voyage of the Dawn Treader*. New York: HarperCollins Publishers, 1994.

Tampon activism: Zraick, Karen. "It's Not Just the Tampon Tax: Why Periods Are Political." *New York Times*, July 22, 2018. https://www.nytimes.com/2018/07 /22/health/tampon-tax-periods-menstruation-nyt.html.

Wang, Esmé Weijun. "I'm Chronically Ill and Afraid of Being Lazy." *ELLE*, April 26, 2016. https://www.elle.com/life-love/a35930/chronically-ill-afraid-lazy.

THAT'S WHAT YOU THINK

Regier, Willis Goth. *Book of the Sphinx*. Lincoln: University of Nebraska Press, 2007.

Rukeyser, Muriel, *The Collected Poems of Muriel Rukeyser*. University of Pittsburgh Press, 2005. Edited by Janet E. Kaufman and Anne F. Herzog. http://muriel rukeyser.emuenglish.org/2018/12/07/myth.

Second riddle: Wright, Matthew. *The Lost Plays of Greek Tragedy (Volume 1): Neglected Authors*. London: Bloomsbury Academic, 2016.

DEEP HOUSES

House on the Rock details: Jordan, Alex, and Dick Schneck. *The House on the Rock*. Spring Green, WI: House on the Rock Publishing, 1976.

D&D chimeras: Wizards of the Coast. *Dungeons & Dragons Monster Manual*. Renton, WA: Wizards of the Coast, 2014.

Microchimerism: Svitil, Kathy A. "You Are a Chimera (Thanks to Mom)." *Discover*, May 9, 2007. http://discovermagazine.com/2007/may/we-are-all -chimeras.

X-inactivation: Migeon, Barbara R. *Females Are Mosaics: X Inactivation and Sex Differences in Disease*. New York: Oxford University Press, 2013.

Zimmerman, Jess. "'Where's My Cut?': On Unpaid Emotional Labor." *The Toast*, July 13, 2015. http://the-toast.net/2015/07/13/emotional-labor.

"Emotional Labor: The MetaFilter Thread Condensed." Prepared by Josh Millard, January 15, 2016. http://www.victorkumar.org/uploads/6/1/5/2/61526489 /emotional_labor_-_the_metafilter_thread_condensed-.pdf.

Emotion work as more gendered than other household work: Erickson, Rebecca J. "Why Emotion Work Matters: Sex, Gender, and the Division of Household Labor." *Journal of Marriage and Family*, April 2005. https://doi.org/10.1111/j.0022 -2445.2005.00120.x.

Pliny the Elder. *Pliny's Natural History in Thirty-Seven Books*. Translated by Philemon Holland. Archive. London: Printed for the Club by G. Barclay, 1847–49. Digitized by the University of California Libraries. https://archive.org/details /plinysnaturalhis00plinrich/page/n8.

Strayed, Cheryl. "Dear Sugar, the Rumpus Advice Column #77: The Truth That Lives There." *The Rumpus*, June 24, 2011. https://therumpus.net/2011/06/dear -sugar-the-rumpus-advice-column-77-the-truth-that-lives-there.

THE SNATCHERS

Virgil. *The Aeneid*, Translated by John Dryden, 1697. New York: P.F. Collier and Son, 1909. https://oll.libertyfund.org/titles/virgil-the-aeneid-dryden-trans.

Herbert, Ian. "Are These American Stars Too Arrogant? Even France Will Be Backing England." *Daily Mail Online*, June 30, 2019. https://www.dailymail.co.uk /sport/football/article-7198249/Are-American-stars-arrogant-France-backing -England.html.

Trump vs. Rapinoe: Fabian, Jordan. "Trump Blasts Rapinoe: 'Megan Should Win First Before She Talks.'" *The Hill*, June 26, 2019. https://thehill.com/homenews /administration/450417-trump-blasts-rapinoe-megan-should-win-first-before -she-talks.

Trump vs. the Squad: Rogers, Katie, and Nicholas Fandos. "Trump Tells Congresswomen to 'Go Back' to the Countries They Came From." *New York Times*, July 14, 2019. https://www.nytimes.com/2019/07/14/us/politics/trump-twitter -squad-congress.html.

AOC and Rapinoe vs. Trump: Resto-Montero, Gabriela. "Ocasio-Cortez Invites the US Women's Soccer Team to the House of Representatives." *Vox*, June 29, 2019. https://www.vox.com/2019/6/29/19953294/ocasio-cortez-megan -rapinoe-us-womens-soccer-team-house-representatives.

Female MBAs downplaying achievements: Bursztyn, Leonardo, et al. "'Acting Wife': Marriage Market Incentives and Labor Market Investments." *American Economic Review*, 2017. https://scholar.harvard.edu/pallais/publications/acting -wife-marriage-market-incentives-and-labor-market-investments.

Ambition gap in politics: Fox, Richard L., and Jennifer L. Lawless. "Why Are Women Still Not Running for Public Office?" *Brookings*, July 28, 2016. https:// www.brookings.edu/research/why-are-women-still-not-running-for-public -office.

Reaction to "power-seeking" women: Okimoto, Tyler G., and Victoria L. Brescoll. "The Price of Power: Power Seeking and Backlash Against Female Politicians." *Personality and Social Psychology Bulletin* 36, no. 7 (June 2, 2010): 923–36. http:// gap.hks.harvard.edu/price-power-power-seeking-and-backlash-against-female -politicians.

Sad and Rabid Puppies trying to game the Hugos: Robinson, Tasha. "How the Sad Puppies Won—By Losing." NPR, August 26, 2015. https://www.npr.org/2015 /08/26/434644645/how-the-sad-puppies-won-by-losing.

More Puppies: Walter, Damien. "Diversity Wins as the Sad Puppies Lose at the Hugo Awards." *The Guardian*, August 24, 2015. https://www.theguardian.com /books/booksblog/2015/aug/24/diversity-wins-as-the-sad-puppies-lose-at-the -hugo-awards.

Vox Day being awful: Day, Vox. "Pink SF vs Blue SF." *Vox Popoli*, December 4, 2013. https://voxday.blogspot.com/2013/12/pink-sf-vs-blue-sf.html.

Chen, Karissa. "They All Laughed at Edwidge Danticat." *Electric Literature*, December 6, 2017. https://electricliterature.com/they-all-laughed-at-edwidge -danticat.

All-male abortion panel: Bassett, Laura. "20-Week Abortion Bill Advanced by All-Male Congressional Panel." *Huffington Post*, June 5, 2013. https://www .huffpost.com/entry/20-week-abortion-bill_n_3385122.

Pence's all-male health bill meeting: "All-Male White House Health Bill Photo Sparks Anger." *BBC News*, March 24, 2017. https://www.bbc.com/news /world-us-canada-39375228.

All-male contraception hearing: Zornick, George. "Republican Hearing on Contraception: No Women Allowed." *The Nation*, June 29, 2015. https://www .thenation.com/article/republican-hearing-contraception-no-women-allowed.

Male politicians making decisions for women: Clayton, Amanda, et al. "Americans Don't Like It When Men (and Only Men) Make Decisions About Women." *Washington Post*, April 4, 2017. https://www.washingtonpost.com/news/monkey -cage/wp/2017/04/04/americans-dont-like-it-when-men-and-only-men-make -decisions-about-women.

Incels: Tolentino, Jia. "The Rage of the Incels." *New Yorker*, May 15, 2018. https:// www.newyorker.com/culture/cultural-comment/the-rage-of-the-incels.

Vultures: Associated Press. "Vomiting Vultures Completely Take Over Couple's Luxury Vacation Home." *HuffPost*, August 16, 2019. https://www.huffpost .com/entry/vomiting-vultures-florida-vacation-home_n_5d56fc6ee4b056fafd 0ba527.

SOCIAL JUSTICE WARRIORS

Sting pain scale: Schmidt, Justin O. *The Sting of the Wild*. Baltimore, MD: Johns Hopkins University Press, 2016.

Chthonic symbolism: Felton, Debbie. "Rejecting and Embracing the Monstrous in Ancient Greece and Rome." *The Ashgate Research Companion to Monsters and the Monstrous*. Edited by Asa Simon Mittman and Peter J. Dendle. New York: Ashgate, 2013.

Aeschylus, *The Oresteia of Aeschylus*. Translated by Robert Lowell. New York: Farrar, Straus & Giroux, 1978.

Gender bias in jury deliberation: Arizona State University. "Angry Men Gain Influence, Angry Women Lose Influence, Study Shows." *Science Daily*, October 26, 2015. https://www.sciencedaily.com/releases/2015/10/151026172546.htm.

Isla Vista killings: Poston, Ben. "Killer Who Committed Massacre in Isla Vista Was Part of Alt-Right, New Research Shows." *Los Angeles Times*, February 6, 2018. https://www.latimes.com/local/lanow/la-me-isle-vista-massacre-alt-right -20180206-story.html.

Bill Cosby accusations: Malone, Noreen, and Amanda Demme. "'I'm No Longer Afraid': 35 Women Tell Their Stories About Being Assaulted by Bill Cosby, and the Culture That Wouldn't Listen." *The Cut*, July 27, 2015. https://www.thecut .com/2015/07/bill-cosbys-accusers-speak-out.html.

Brock Turner case: Miller, Chanel. *Know My Name: A Memoir*. New York: Viking, 2019.

Brock Turner victim impact statement: Baker, Katie J. M. "Here's the Powerful Letter the Stanford Victim Read to Her Attacker." *BuzzFeed News*, June 3, 2016. https://www.buzzfeednews.com/article/katiejmbaker/heres-the-powerful -letter-the-stanford-victim-read-to-her-ra.

Weinstein accusations: Kantor, Jodi, and Megan Twohey. "Harvey Weinstein Paid Off Sexual Harassment Accusers for Decades." *New York Times*, October 5, 2017. https://www.nytimes.com/2017/10/05/us/harvey-weinstein-harassment -allegations.html.

Weinstein again: Farrow, Ronan. "From Aggressive Overtures to Sexual Assault: Harvey Weinstein's Accusers Tell Their Stories." *New Yorker*, August 22, 2019. https://www.newyorker.com/news/news-desk/from-aggressive-overtures-to -sexual-assault-harvey-weinsteins-accusers-tell-their-stories.

Roy Moore accusations: Bump, Philip. "Timeline: The Accusations Against Roy Moore." *Washington Post*, November 16, 2017. https://www.washingtonpost.com /news/politics/wp/2017/11/16/timeline-the-accusations-against-roy-moore/.

Louis C.K. accusations: Ryzik, Melena, et al. "Louis C.K. Is Accused by 5 Women of Sexual Misconduct." *New York Times*, November 9, 2017. https://www. nytimes.com/2017/11/09/arts/television/louis-ck-sexual-misconduct.html.

Chris Hardwick accusation: Dykstra, Chloe. "Rose-Colored Glasses: A Confession." *Medium*, July 7, 2018. https://medium.com/@skydart/rose-colored-glasses -6be0594970ca.

Ryan Adams accusations: Kreps, Daniel. "Ryan Adams Accused of Sexual Misconduct, Emotional Abuse by Seven Women." *Rolling Stone*, February 14, 2019.

https://www.rollingstone.com/music/music-news/ryan-adams-accused-of
-sexual-misconduct-emotional-abuse-by-seven-women-794117.

#MeToo: Burke, Tarana. "#MeToo Founder Tarana Burke on the Rigorous Work That Still Lies Ahead." *Variety*, January 24, 2019. https://variety.com/2018/biz /features/tarana-burke-metoo-one-year-later-1202954797.

Loofbourow, Lili. "Everyone Got to Be Angry at the Kavanaugh Hearing Except Christine Blasey Ford." *Slate*, September 29, 2018. https://slate.com/news-and -politics/2018/09/brett-kavanaugh-hearing-angry-shouting.html.

Elliot Rodger as an incel role model: "Elliot Rodger: How Misogynist Killer Became 'Incel Hero.'" *BBC News*, April 26, 2018. https://www.bbc.com/news /world-us-canada-43892189.

Roy Moore doesn't stay down: Blinder, Alan. "Roy Moore to Run for Alabama Senate Seat Again." *New York Times*, June 20, 2019. https://www.nytimes.com /2019/06/20/us/politics/roy-moore-running-again.html.

Hardwick comeback: Bradley, Bill. "Chris Hardwick Returns to 'Talking Dead'; Staffers Resign." *HuffPost*, August 13, 2018. https://www.huffpost.com/entry /chris-hardwick-talking-dead_n_5b6b473be4b0530743c69be7.

C.K. comeback: Grady, Constance. "Louis C.K.'s Controversial Comeback Attempt, Explained." *Vox*, September 5, 2018. https://www.vox.com/culture/2018/9 /5/17820346/louis-ck-comedy-cellar-comeback-workplace-safety.

Law, Victoria. "How Many Women Are in Prison for Defending Themselves Against Domestic Violence?" *Bitch*, September 16, 2014. https://www.bitch media.org/post/women-in-prison-for-fighting-back-against-domestic-abuse -ray-rice.

West, Lindy. "Brave Enough to Be Angry." *New York Times*, November 8, 2017. https://www.nytimes.com/2017/11/08/opinion/anger-women-weinstein -assault.html.

Anger at misogyny affecting health: Strapagiel, Lauren. "Everyday Acts of Discrimination May Raise Women's Blood Pressure over Time." *BuzzFeed News*, October 11, 2018. https://www.buzzfeednews.com/article/laurenstrapagiel /discrimination-linked-high-blood-pressure-women.

Anger at racism affecting health: Mays, Vickie M., et al. "Race, Race-Based Discrimination, and Health Outcomes Among African Americans." *Annual Review of Psychology*, 2007. https://www.ncbi.nlm.nih.gov/pmc/articles/PMC4181672.

Anger at classism affecting health: Simons, Audrey M. W., et al. "Perceived Classism and Its Relation with Socioeconomic Status, Health, Health Behaviours and Perceived Inferiority: The Dutch Longitudinal Internet Studies for the Social Sciences (LISS) Panel." *International Journal of Public Health*, 2017. https://www .ncbi.nlm.nih.gov/pmc/articles/PMC5397436/.

Anger at weight discrimination affecting health: Tomiyama, A. Janet, et al. "How and Why Weight Stigma Drives the Obesity 'Epidemic' and Harms Health." *BMC Medicine*, August 15, 2018.

Sexual abusers rarely convicted: Block, Stephanie D., and Linda M. Williams. "The Prosecution of Child Sexual Abuse: A Partnership to Improve Outcomes." *National Criminal Justice Reference Service*, US Department of Justice, March 2019. https://www.ncjrs.gov/pdffiles1/nij/grants/252768.pdf.

SINGING FOR BREAD

Atwood, Margaret. *You Are Happy*. New York: Oxford University Press, 1974. https://www.poetryfoundation.org/poetrymagazine/poems/32778/siren-song.
Shakespeare, William, *Hamlet*, New York: Signet Classics, 1998.

COME BACK TWICE AS HARD

Ovid. *Heroides and Amores*. Translated by Grant Showerman and G. P. Goold. Cambridge, MA: Harvard University Press, 1914.
Penny, Laurie. "Non-Compete Clause." *The Baffler*, January 15, 2018. https://thebaffler.com/war-of-nerves/non-compete.
Weinstein accusations: See *Monstrous Anger*.
Killingsworth, Silvia. "You Can't Get Away with This Shit Anymore." *The Awl*, October 11, 2017. https://www.theawl.com/2017/10/you-cant-get-away-with-this-shit-anymore.
Shafrir, Doree. "What to Do with 'Shitty Media Men'?" *BuzzFeed News*, October 12, 2017. https://www.buzzfeednews.com/article/doree/what-to-do-with-shitty-media-men.
Ryan, Lisa. "BuzzFeed Fires White House Correspondent Who Appeared on Media Men List." *The Cut*, December 27, 2017. https://www.thecut.com/2017/12/buzzfeed-fires-adrian-carrasquillo-white-house.html.
Schuessler, Jennifer. "Leon Wieseltier Admits 'Offenses' Against Female Colleagues as New Magazine Is Killed." *New York Times*, October 24, 2017. https://www.nytimes.com/2017/10/24/arts/leon-wieseltier-magazine-harassment.html.
Alter, Alexandra, and Sydney Ember. "Paris Review Editor Resigns Amid Inquiry into His Conduct with Women." *New York Times*, December 6, 2017. https://www.nytimes.com/2017/12/06/books/lorin-stein-resigns-the-paris-review.html.
Bosman, Julie. "Lorin Stein, Editor of The Paris Review." *New York Times*, February 25, 2011. http://www.nytimes.com/2011/02/27/fashion/27Stein.html.
Donegan, Moira. "I Started the Media Men List." *The Cut*, January 11, 2018. https://www.thecut.com/2018/01/moira-donegan-i-started-the-media-men-list.html.
Crenshaw, Kimberlé. "Demarginalizing the Intersection of Race and Sex: A Black Feminist Critique of Antidiscrimination Doctrine, Feminist Theory and Anti-racist Politics." *University of Chicago Legal Forum* (1989): 139–68.
Adewunmi, Bim. "Kimberlé Crenshaw on Intersectionality: 'I Wanted to Come Up with an Everyday Metaphor That Anyone Could Use.'" *New Statesman America*, April 2, 2014. https://www.newstatesman.com/lifestyle/2014/04/kimberl-crenshaw-intersectionality-i-wanted-come-everyday-metaphor-anyone-could.
Kendall, Mikki. "#SolidarityIsForWhiteWomen: Women of Color's Issue with Digital Feminism." *Guardian*, August 14, 2013. https://www.theguardian.com/commentisfree/2013/aug/14/solidarityisforwhitewomen-hashtag-feminism.

SHARK, SNAKE, SWARM

Bell, Robert E. *Women of Classical Mythology: A Biographical Dictionary*. Santa Barbara, CA: ABC-CLIO, 1991.
Ogden, Daniel. *Dragons, Serpents, and Slayers in the Classical and Early Christian Worlds: A Sourcebook*. New York: Oxford University Press, 2013.

Keats, John. "Lamia." https://www.gutenberg.org/files/2490/2490-h/2490-h.htm. Originally published 1819.

Abortion frequency: Planned Parenthood, *2017–2018 Annual Report*. https://www .plannedparenthood.org/uploads/filer_public/4a/0f/4a0f3969-cf71–4ec3–8a90 –733c01ee8148/190124-annualreport18-p03.pdf.

Percentage of people who get abortions who are already mothers: Singh, Susheela, et al. *Abortion Worldwide 2017: Uneven Progress and Unequal Access*. Guttmacher Institute. https://www.guttmacher.org/report/abortion-worldwide-2017.

#ShoutYourAbortion: West, Lindy. "I Set Up #ShoutYourAbortion Because I Am Not Sorry, and I Will Not Whisper." *The Guardian*, September 22, 2015. https://www.theguardian.com/commentisfree/2015/sep/22/i-set-up-shoutyour abortion-because-i-am-not-sorry-and-i-will-not-whisper.

More #ShoutYourAbortion: Lewin, Tamar. "#ShoutYourAbortion Gets Angry Shouts Back." *New York Times*, October 1, 2015. https://www.nytimes.com /2015/10/02/us/hashtag-campaign-twitter-abortion.html.

CREDITS

"How to Turn a Man to Stone" is adapted from "What If We Cultivated Our Ugliness? or: The Monstrous Beauty of Medusa," published in *Catapult*, May 23, 2017.

"Voracious" is adapted from "Hunger Makes Me," published in *Hazlitt*, July 7, 2016.

"The Snatchers" is adapted from "The Monstrous Female Ambition of the Harpy," published in *Catapult*, April 24, 2017.

"Social Justice Warriors" is adapted from "Anger That Can Save the World: On Justice, Feminism, and the Furies," published in *Catapult*, August 30, 2017.

"Deep Houses" is adapted from "Claim Your Complexity: The Monstrous Upheaval of the Chimera," published in *Catapult*, June 27, 2017.

"Shark, Snake, Swarm" is adapted from "When It Is Considered Monstrous Not to Want Children, and Monstrous to Want Them Too Much," published in *Catapult*, July 31, 2017.

ABOUT THE AUTHOR

JESS ZIMMERMAN is an editor, an essayist, an occasional fiction writer, and a former opinion columnist, journalist, and academic (not at the same time). She is the coauthor, with Jaya Saxena, of *Basic Witches*.

SAMIRA INGOLD can be found on Instagram at @__ra.in__. She lives in Switzerland.